CHRISTIANITY
AND THE
AMERICAN
COMMONWEALTH

CHRISTIANITY
AND THE
AMERICAN
COMMONWEALTH

OR

*The Influence of Christianity in
Making This Nation*

By

BISHOP CHARLES B. GALLOWAY, D.D, LL.D.

Delivered in the Chapel at Emory College, Oxford, GA.,
March, 1898

American Vision, Inc.
POWDER SPRINGS, GEORGIA

American Vision

A Biblical Worldview Ministry

www.AmericanVision.org • 1-800-628-9460

© 2005 by American Vision, Inc. All rights reserved.
Published May 2005.
Second Printing December 2005.
Third Printing August 2007.
Fourth Printing April 2008.

Printed in the United States of America.

Note: Misspellings and typographical errors have been corrected. In addition, subheadings have been added and occasional minor editorial revisions have been made to Galloway's text to clarify the material for the modern reader.

American Vision
3150-A Florence Road, SW
Powder Springs, Georgia 30127

Cover artwork: *The Signing of the Mayflower Compact*

Cover design by Luis Lovelace

Library of Congress Cataloging-in-Publication Data
Galloway, Charles B. Christianity and the American Commonwealth
Includes an introduction by Gary DeMar

ISBN: 0–915815–72–9

1. History 2. Religion (Christianity) 3. Church / State

Contents

INTRODUCTION

BY GARY DeMAR

CHARLES BETTS GALLOWAY (1849–1909) was born in Kosciusko, Mississippi, September 1, 1849. His early schooling came by way of private tutoring. At fourteen he attended a school for boys in Canton, and at sixteen he entered the University of Mississippi as a sophomore. He became a Christian during a revival at the university and later felt called to preach the gospel. His first pastorate was in Jackson. After serving four years in Jackson, he began a four-year pastorate in Vicksburg in what was the strongest church in the Mississippi Conference at that time. The character and pastoral heart of Charles Galloway became evident during a yellow fever epidemic in 1878.

> Galloway and his wife remained in the city and daily served the sick and the dying. Contracting the disease, both became desperately ill, and the physician, believing that Galloway was near death, permitted friends to bring his wife on a mattress to his side for their last words together. When the kindly neighbors returned to the room, Galloway said, "I am willing and ready to go, but I cannot think I will go at this time. I have much work yet to do."[1]

Galloway recovered and continued to pastor and take on the additional responsibility of the editorship of the *New*

Orleans Christian Advocate. At the age of 36, he became the youngest man ever elected a bishop in American Methodism. In his ministerial capacity, he made so many official tours of the Orient and South America that he earned the title of "missionary bishop of Methodism." He was also a popular preacher, lecturer, and a famous temperance leader in his day.

Galloway spoke out on racial relationships in a time when there were few reasonable and passionate voices on the subject. His address on "The South and the Negro" was delivered at the seventh annual conference for education in the South, at Birmingham, Alabama, on April 26, 1904. During his speaking tour through Mississippi, Booker T. Washington mentions in his book *My Larger Education* that Galloway was in attendance at one of his meetings:

> Everywhere, I found the greatest interest and enthusiasm among both the white people and coloured people for the work that we were attempting to do. In Jackson, which for a number of years had been the centre of agitation upon the Negro question, there was some opposition expressed to the white people of the town attending the meeting, but I was told that among the people in the audience were Governor Noel; Lieutenant-Governor Manship; Major R. W. Milsaps, who is said to be the wealthiest man in Mississippi; Bishop Charles B. Galloway, of the Methodist Episcopal Church (South), who has since died; United States Marshal Edgar S. Wilson; the postmaster of Jackson, and a number of other prominent persons.[2]

Bishop Galloway understood the importance of Christian higher education. He was a trustee of the University of Mississippi from 1882–1894 and served as President of the board of trustees of Vanderbilt University from 1905 until his death in 1909.

Galloway's world travels brought him into contact with other cultures and their worldviews. He saw the effects of false religion on whole civilizations. His arguments in *Christianity and the American Commonwealth*, although written more than 100 years ago, are persuasively modern and need to be heeded by today's church. He counters the mistaken notion that God's Word is a one-dimensional devotional guide:

> They fatally undervalue the mighty mission of Christianity who limit it merely to "the assertion of moral principle," without any care for its social and political results. It contemplates the sanctification of the home, the redemption of the nation, the purification of commerce, and the exaltation of civic virtue. When our Lord announced that his kingdom is not of this world, he meant not to say that it had nothing to do with the things of this world. His mission was to adjust human relations; and the enthronement of his gospel is the life of society that will right all social wrongs and bring in a new heaven and a new earth. The teachings of Christ are the perfect solution of all the problems of society.[3]

Galloway was forward thinking enough to understand how the media impact society. In a speech to the National Editorial Association, meeting in Jackson, Mississippi, in 1899, Galloway declared of the press: "Along with the family, the church and the state, and not inferior to either because affecting each, it ranks as a dominant force in all civilizations....The press is 'the mightiest of the mighty means, on which the arms of progress leans....What the eloquent tongue of Tully was to Rome, and the impassioned periods of Demosthenes to Athenian patriotism, the modern press is to American citizenship."[4]

The five lectures that appear in this new edition of *Christianity and the American Commonwealth* were first delivered in the Chapel at Emory College, Oxford, Georgia, in March of 1898. The purpose of the series was "to promote the cause of Christian education and to advance the theological literature of Methodism." The lecture series was funded by W. F. Quillian, and came to be regarded as "The Quillian Lectureship."

Galloway's book is one of the best summaries of the impact of Christianity on America. He leaves no stone unturned in his historical and logical arguments to demonstrate that without the gospel and the application of all of God's Word to all of life, civilizations turn despotic and crumble. His closing words are as true today as they were in 1898: "Correct principles sown in the soil of the young mind, cultivated by wise, well-equipped teachers, and ripened by the sun of a gracious Providence, will produce a manhood and womanhood that will sacredly preserve the past and guarantee the glory of the future."[5]

In order to enhance the narrative, American Vision has added subheads and more than a 100 images from its extensive image library.

Notes

1. J. B. Cain, "Charles Betts Calloway," *The Encyclopedia of World Methodism*, ed. Nolan B. Harmon, 2 vols. (Nashville: United Methodist Publishing House, 1974), 893.

2. Booker T. Washington, *My Larger Education* (Garden City, NY: Doubleday, Page, & Co., 1911), 196.

3. Charles B. Galloway, *Christianity and the American Commonwealth; or, The Influence of Christianity in Making this Nation* (Nashville, TN: Publishing House Methodist Episcopal Church, South, 1898), 13 (new edition, 3–4).

4. Quoted in Hodding Carter III, "Giving New Life to a Free Society," American Society of Newspaper Editors (April 12, 2004): www.asne.org/index.cfm?ID=5266

5. Galloway, *Christianity and the American Commonwealth*, 213 (new edition, 169).

CHAPTER 1

Religion and Civil Government

IN ACCEPTING THE kindly worded invitation of the Board of Trustees to inaugurate the series of lectures on the Quillian foundation in this historic institution, I must first express my high appreciation of the ecclesiastical statesmanship and wise beneficence displayed by the worthy founder. Similar foundations in the great universities of Europe and America have become thrones of power, and have already made valuable contributions to the literature of Christian doctrine and apologetics. They have enriched the thought and stimulated the faith of the modern Church. It gave me joy, therefore, to hear that a lectureship had been established in this college, and my hope is that it may take rank with others as a place of authority in high scholarship and Christian culture. And this ardent hope occasioned my extreme reluctance to appear here to-day. Unaffectedly conscious of my lack of qualification for a service of this character, I should have positively declined but for the terms in which the invitation was conveyed.

The theme chosen for this series of chapters is: *Christianity and the American Commonwealth; or, The Influence of Christianity in Making This Nation.*

SYMBOLS OF AMERICA'S FIRST 100 YEARS

I wish it borne in mind that this is to be in no sense a study of Church history. I have no purpose to trace the growth of ecclesiastical organizations, or the progress of Christianity in the United States. The object of this discussion is to ascertain how far the type of religion embraced by the American colonists affected and determined the character of our civil institutions and the course of our social progress. It is not personal but civic righteousness with which we are immediately concerned; not religion as it achieves the salvation of the soul, but religion as it exalts the nation; not so much spiritual as social and civil redemption.

GEORGIA STATE CONSTITUTION (1777):

"We, the people of Georgia, relying upon protection and guidance of Almighty God, do ordain and establish this constitution."

I shall have little to do with the statistics of Churches, and more with the constitutions of commonwealths, the statutes of states, and the history of jurisprudence. Our investigation will be along the line of that approved statement of Kidd, in his *Social Evolution:* "After all, Christianity was intended to save not only men but man, and its mission should be to teach us not only how to die as individuals but how to live as members of society."

The Christian design for the world is not "an anarchy of good individuals." They fatally undervalue the mighty mission of Christianity who limit it merely to "the assertion of moral principle," without any care for its social and political results. It contemplates the sanctification of the home, the redemption of the nation, the purification of commerce, and the exaltation of civic virtue. When our Lord announced that his kingdom is not of this world, he meant not to say that it had nothing to do with the things of this world. His mission was to adjust human relations; and the enthronement of his gospel in the life of society will right all social wrongs and bring in a new heaven and a new earth. The teachings of Christ are the perfect solution of all the problems of society. Mr.

WILLIAM GLADSTONE

Gladstone, at once a statesman and a seer, spoke words of truth and soberness, though with spiritual energy, when he said: "Talk about the questions of the day: there is but one question, and that is the gospel. It can and will correct everything needing correction."

And I feel also that an apology is due because of the subject selected for these lectures. Though the study of history has for years had for me a strange fascination, I have no such special expert acquaintance with its facts or philosophy as to entitle me to speak by the authority of accurate and ample knowledge. The exacting and laborious duties of my responsible office, necessitating wearisome travel at home and abroad, and bereaving me of the delightful proviliges of a library for weeks at a time, afford little opportunity for prosecuting any definite line of investigation. I can only hope, therefore, to offer some suggestions that may stimulate other students to fully explore a much-neglected field.

The Minimization of Religion in History

To the study of this subject I have been impelled by the evident tendency of some modern historians to minify, if not almost entirely eliminate, religion from the formative forces of our American institutions. Books on the making of our nation have been written, and are the texts in our colleges, in which the Christian religion, as a social and civil factor, has only scant or apologetic mention. This is either a fatal oversight or a deliberate purpose, and both alike are to be

deplored and condemned. A nation ashamed of its ancestry will be despised by its posterity. Whatever use or misuse we may make of our inheritance, it is well to be reminded from whence it came. We ought to know the genesis of our institutions, though we may have to lament their exodus. With the growth of a subtle materialistic spirit which invades every department of life, however sacred and secret, we are threatened with an undervaluing or ignoring of the great moral and spiritual forces that constructed the massive framework of this mighty nation. Climatic, economic,

COLUMBUS GIVING THANKS UPON REACHING THE NEW WORLD

racial, and purely political forces are analyzed and properly classified; but the religious factor, which more than either or all of them determined the character of our civilization and the form of our government, has received very indifferent, if not malevolent, consideration. All of which confirms the judgment of a distinguished writer who has recently observed that "the place of religion in human history is too often the subject merely of ecclesiastical or antiecclesiastical declamation, or else, through fear of giving offense, it is left severely alone."

Now, with the hope of contributing somewhat to the arrest of that tendency, and of aiding the students of this honored institution to a broader study of the earlier history of this American commonwealth, I have timidly ventured upon the theme of these lectures. My purpose shall be, if possible, to demonstrate that Protestant Christianity has been the dominent influence in our nation's construction and continuation. For I hesitate not to affirm that the temple at Jerusalem was built by a no more sacred patriotism or under the benedictions of a no more favoring Providence than were the colonial governments of this New World.

SOLOMON'S TEMPLE

Christian teachings were the seed-thoughts of our political constitutions, and Christian evangelism was the inspiration of American colonization. If we eliminate from our national history the direct and all-powerful influence of the Christian religion, we have nothing left but a set of disjointed facts without significance, dry and dreary annals without parentage or posterity. But, on the other hand, a right apprehension of all the formative forces in our national life will vindicate the matured judgment of Emerson, that "our whole history appears like a last effort of Divine Providence in behalf of the human race."

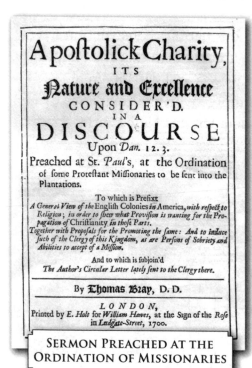

SERMON PREACHED AT THE ORDINATION OF MISSIONARIES

Religion and Civil Government

Now, as introductory to this study of our earlier American history, and in order to get a vantage point from which to take the most satisfactory observations, I shall speak to-day on the general subject of RELIGION AND CIVIL GOVERNMENT. My contention will be that the governments and civilizations of all people are typed and determined by the character of their religions. And this proposition will hold good whether the religion be true or false. The deepest and mightiest thing in any nation's heart is its religion; therefore as is the religion so is the nation. "The kingdom of heaven is within you," some one once quoted to Frederick Maurice. "Yes," he replied, "and so is the kingdom of England." And to every true American we may say, "And so is the republic of the United States." Now if this discussion shall prove to be a demonstration, the application of these clearly ascertained principles to our American commonwealth will account for the history and reveal the true philosophy of our social and civil institutions.

There is an intimate, a vital connection between the spiritual and political faiths of a people. As God hath joined them together, they can not be put asunder. So intimate indeed is this relation that the dominance of the one determines the characteer of the other. The heavens and the earth are in immediate and vital relation. And no people can have politically a new earth until they have first had spiritually a new heaven. On this point the distinguished Dr. Fairbairn has thus spoken:

> Political thought is the religious idea applied to the state and the conduct of its public affairs, while religious thought is but our view of the polity of the universe, and man's relation to it. It follows that as man thinks in the one field he comes to think also in the other.

But I should go farther, and say that a man's thinking in the political field is invariably, if not necessarily, determined by his convictions in the spiritual field. In the realm of the civil, as in the ecclesiastical, the old aphorism holds good: "Like priest, like people." The state is a true reflex of the Church; the civil law is a faithful rescript of the canon law. And, as in the days of the Hebrew theocracy, so in all lands and under all religions, there is a close connection between the sanctuary and the seat of judgment. The altar shapes the throne, the character of the crozier measures the strength of the scepter. Out of religious doctrines are developed political principles; and, therefore, the purer the religion the broader a nation's constitution and the wiser its civil polity. Religion is a political force as well as a spiritual influence; both a social dynamic and a celestial inspiration. With a slight modification I accept the statement of Prof.

Seeley: "From history we learn that the great function of religion has been the founding and sustaining of states." And in language quite as emphatic that accomplished student on another occasion expressed the same critical judgment as follows: "Look almost where you will in the wide field

ROUSSEAU

of history, you find religion, wherever it works freely and mightily, either giving birth to and sustaining states, or else raising them up to a second life after their destruction." And even the skeptical but philosophically acute and observant Rousseau, himself a political leader and social reformer, gives assent to the same great doctrine in these strong words: "Never was a state founded that did not have religion for its basis."

History and Religion in Government

All the civil institutions of the ancient world were the outgrowth of religious belief, the social expressions of a spiritual faith. Nations were governed as the gods directed. Kings ruled, judges delivered opinions, soldiers fought, generals planned their campaigns, all under the patronage and supposed guidance of their favorite deities. Oracles were consulted, shrines were reverently visited, and costly sacrifices freely offered, in order to secure the approval of the gods before any movement was undertaken. The Roman Empire, whether pagan or Christian, from Romulus to

Charlemagne, "never dreamed of executing its functions without a divinity." "The Greek king" as a distinguished

CHARLEMAGNE

scholar has said, "pronounced his decisions as judge by inspiration from Themis. The Roman king learned the elements of legislation from the nymph Egeria." The Mohammedan power, swift and terrible as an avalanche, and cruel as death itself, "made religion the most vigorous element in its administration, civil and military." And the history of the Hebrew nation teaches with powerful emphasis and endless iteration the imminence of their God. "The theocracy in Israel," as Canon Freemantle well says, "was the righteous God abiding in the nation. The theocracy in Christendom was to be the same righteous power abiding in mankind."

Heathen and Christian alike, in all ages of the world, have regarded religion as the basis of the commonwealth, as the very condition of national existence. Those were remarkable words uttered by Plutarch, one of the greatest and purest disciples of Plato:

PLUTARCH

> There never was a state of atheists. You may travel all over the world, and you may find cities without walls, without king, without mint, without theater or gymnasium; but you will nowhere find a city without a God, without prayer, without oracle, without sacrifice. Sooner may a city

stand without foundations than a state without belief in the gods. This is the bond of all society and the pillar of all legislation.

All history attests to the fact that religion is not only a helpful influence, but that it is the most potential factor in a nation's life. Governments could not exist without its cohesive and undergirding power. Their steadiest support would be withdrawn, their mightiest bulwark dismantled. And all far-seeing rulers, without regard to their own personal feelings or opinions, have not failed to take this fundamental fact into account. Speaking of religion as a national force, as "the mystery of social order," Napoleon said: "One can not govern without it; otherwise the repose, dignity, and independence of the nation are disturbed at every moment." And in historic support of the doctrine here announced, this great master of statecraft further observed:

NAPOLEON

In the Roman republic the senate was the interpreter of heaven, and this was the mainspring of the force and strength of that government. In Turkey, and throughout the Orient, the Koran serves as both a civil and religious Bible. Only in Christianity do we find the pontificate distinct from civil government.

Religion and Civil Law

Lord Erskine, England's great constitutional lawyer and forensic orator, in prosecuting a man charged with high crime, thus referred to the cohesive power of our Christian religion: "Depend upon it, the world can not be held together without morals; nor can morals maintain their station in the human heart without religion, which is the corner-stone of the fabric of human virtue." And the distinguished Chief Justice of this great state of Georgia, the Hon. Joseph H. Lumpkin, has with equal eloquence and force applied the same principle to our American commonwealth:

> Banish the Bible from the land, or, what is the same thing, succeed in loosing its hold on the public mind, and my word for it, the experiment of self-government will prove a failure.

Political atheism will inevitably produce political anarchy. For a nation, as for an individual, it is better to have a bad god than no god at all. Kishub Chunder Sen, of India, showed himself a genuine philosopher when he uttered this distressful apprehension: "I fear for my countrymen that they will sink from the hell of heathenism into the deeper hell of infidelity." A nation without a God is a nation without a conscience; and a nation without a conscience knows no rule of right but might, perverts law into license, and makes authority the bitter synonym of cruel tyranny. On this point the late lamented and learned Dr. Philip Schaff spoke these wise words of warning:

The destruction of religion would be the destruction of morality and the ruin of the state. Civil liberty requires for its support religious liberty, and can not prosper without it.

And David Hume, skeptic though he was, yet an impartial

DAVID HUME

historian and philosopher, did not hesitate to make this candid affirmation: "If you find a people without religion, rest assured that they do not differ much from the brute beasts." But this profound political principle, which is slowly working out its predestined results in the history of nations, long ago had more authoritative announcement than any opinion of uninspired man, in these words of the prophet Isaiah: "The nation and the kingdom that will not serve thee shall perish" [Isa. 60:12].

A striking modern illustration of the doctrine for which I am now contending we have in the "Reign of Terror" in France, that bloodiest chapter in the history of a land of revolutions and counter-revolutions. Blatant infidelity precipitated that storm of pitiless fury. The National Assembly passed a

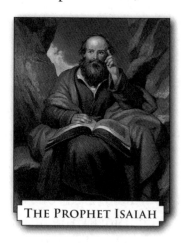

THE PROPHET ISAIAH

resolution deliberately declaring "There is no God;" vacated the throne of Deity by simple resolution, abolished the Sabbath, unfrocked her ministers of religion, turned temples of spiritual worship into places of secular business, and enthroned a vile woman as the Goddess of Reason. Now, instead of larger liberty and wiser laws and more perfect peace and greater commercial and industrial prosperity, the days of anarchy and terror had just begun. That very night the storm burst, and the streets of the world's fairest city ran red with the blood of the proudest chivalry of France. What a verification is that sad history of the eloquent words of Lord

VICTIMS OF THE FRENCH REVOLUTION

Macaulay: "Whoever does anything to depreciate Christianity is guilty of high treason against the civilization of mankind."

The Christian Effect on Civilization

It now becomes necessary to examine somewhat into the civilizations of people living under different religions in order to ascertain how far the principles here announced are verified by the facts of history. If my contention is true, we shall discover that civil governments and their administration differ as their religions differ. That which so powerfully affects the inner life must of necessity determine the outer form of society.

It would be most instructive, if the limits of this discussion allowed, to make an extended study of the pagan civilizations of certain countries antedating the Christian period, and

JESUS PREACHING
TO THE MULTITUDE

then note the changes wrought by the coming and dissemination of the religion of the Man of Galilee. Those marvelous changes were not mere coincidences, but the effects of mighty causes potential in the gospel. In a few centuries the spiritual teachings of the Nazarene dethroned the gods of great nations, revolutionized the social life of many peoples, shifted the shadings on the map of the world, and marked the rise and fall of empires. In spite of persecutions long and bitter, in face of legislation malignant and merciless, armed only with spiritual weapons, the Church moved forward to glorious conquest. "Those were times of awful agony," says the historian, "the two years of Decius, the ten years of Diocletian, when the Roman Empire, shutting the gates of the amphitheater, leaped into the arena face to face with the Christian Church. When those gates were opened, the victorious Church went forth with the baptism of blood on her saintly brow, bearing a new Christian empire in her fair, white arms." But it will be amply sufficient for the purpose of this argument to examine existing civilizations and contrast their dominant forces.

And at the very outset of this investigation one broad generalization may be clearly made: *The governments of all non-Christian countries are despotic.* Whatever the cause,

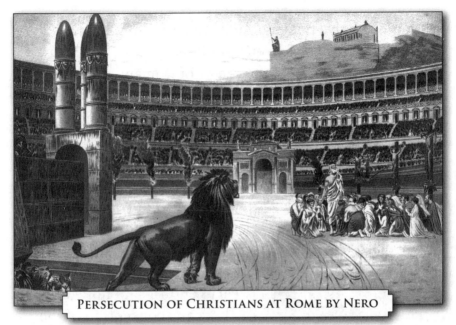

PERSECUTION OF CHRISTIANS AT ROME BY NERO

this is the historic fact, and a fact written in blood and tears. It is a logical and spiritual necessity. A tyrannous religion produces a political despotism. Without spiritual liberty there can be no civil freedom. Dr. Dennis, in his masterly and voluminous work on *Christian Missions and Social Progress*, after a critical and exhaustive survey of the entire field, makes this strong statement: "The history of heathenism is, as a rule, marked by despotism. The old oriental empires and their modern successors are alike in this respect. Savage life has been almost invariably characterized by tyranny on the part of the rulers." And in referring especially to those ill-fated lands under Moslem rule Archbishop Trench makes a like sweeping declaration. He claims that "the despotisms of the East are not accidents, but the legitimate results of the Koran; and so long as this exists

as the authoritative book nothing can come in their stead." Its political supremacy has been a soulless tyranny, wielding a scepter of iron and waving a flag of flame. The civilizations of Japan, China, and India are the social and political expressions of their ancient religions. They have molded the thought, controlled the legislation, and directed the public policies of those vast empires through dreary and weary centuries. In none of them is there any conception of the great doctrine of personal liberty, and only in modern Japan is there an approach to civil and constitutional rights. And a

EXECUTION BY ELEPHANT IN INDIA

like condition of things obtains in the little "hermit nation" of the East. The government of Korea, in the judgment of a native Korean, is "a combination of despotic monarchy and corrupted oligarchy, with the worst elements of both." Its whole machinery is run in the interest of the fewest people at the cruel cost of the nation. Civil oppression, without even a show of justice, was the habit of centuries, and the only hope of the superstitious masses. And to whatever pagan land we turn, the same sad story is heard, a story of heartless tyranny and suffering slaves. The "demon-ridden islands" of the sea, and the dark continent of Africa, with its fetishism and nameless idolatries, only swell the orphan cry of humanity, the weird wail of the millions for that freedom which comes only to those who know the emancipating power of the truth as it is in Jesus.

True Liberty Comes Only from a Christian Worldview

Only in Christian countries do we find liberal and representative government. There autocracies give way to republics, and royal decrees to statutes and constitutions.

LEYDEN, HOLLAND

The old fable of the divine right of kings surrenders to the sovereignty of the people and the reign of constitutional law. I quote again a fine passage from the distinguished Dr. Fairbairn: "If you want political freedom, it is to states that have known what it was to believe in the Christian religion that you must go. You must go to Holland, as she issues purified from her baptism of blood, strengthened in her faith and ennobled in her spirit by the unequal yet victorious struggle against Spain; you must go to England as the Puritans made her; you must go to Scotland as she was made by John Knox; you must go to America, so largely formed, organized, and governed by the sturdy Puritan men of New England and the mild, inflexible Friends and the stalwart Presbyterians of Pennsylvania. And

JOHN KNOX

underneath all you find that the grand, dominant factors are the religious ideas, the faith that came through Jesus Christ."

The social and political force of any religion is measured by the estimate it puts upon *the individual* and *the family*. The religion that enthrones man and sanctifies the home, builds the strongest state, with the surest guarantees of enduring and increasing glory; but, on the other hand, the religion that undervalues the individual and secularizes the home, that disregards personal rights and debases family relationships, of necessity exalts the state into a despotism, degrades the citizen into a mere slave, and breeds immoralities that sooner or later accomplish its ruin. A nation is *strong* in proportion as man is respected as a sovereign and protected in his rights; a nation is *pure* in proportion as the sanctities of the home are properly appreciated and safeguarded.

I shall first, therefore, seek to ascertain what place man holds in the world's great religions, and discover thereby the character of civilization that has been built about him. Every religion must be measured by the man it produces. As is the man so is the religion, and as is the religion so is the nation. I accept without qualification the strong statement of Humboldt, that "governments, religion, property, books, are nothing but the scaffolding to build man. Earth holds up to her Maker no fruit like the finished man."

Non-Christianity Denies the Sanctity of Life

In all non-Christian countries manhood is more or less debased, and human life is cheap. The doctrine that the state must guarantee the protection of life is purely a Christian conception. Kings have put citizens to death to gratify personal revenge, without other authority than their own wills. Dr. Fairbairn states the whole case in a few words: "The great notion in all ancient empires was that the king or the priest owns the people. The idea of man as a conscious, rational, moral individual, of worth

CONFUCIUS

for his own sake, of equal dignity before his Maker, did not exist in antiquity till it came into being through Israel." And that fatal misconception of humanity, distinguishing all non-Christian religions and nations, accounts for the heartless atrocities that so often shock the civilized world and redden the pages of history.

A critical and philosophical student of comparative religions, in estimating their working forces upon individual life and character, has made an analysis which I think eminently correct and just. He finds in Buddhism a paralyzed personality, in Confucianism an impoverished personality, in Hinduism a degraded personality, and in Mohammedism an enslaved personality.

On the other hand, Christianity teaches that every man is a sovereign. It exalts the individual, places the crown of a king upon every human brow, and the crozier of a priest in every human hand. Christ tells us there is nothing greater than

INDIA'S COAT OF ARMS

manhood. In commenting upon the fact that Jesus Christ put value upon man himself, apart from possession or position, James Russell Lowell said he was "the first true democrat that ever breathed."

A paralyzed personality is the legitimate and necessary product of the Buddhist creed. Buddha hated life and preached a gospel of annihilation. His aim was to make men know their misery, that they might willingly escape therefrom. His ultimate and hopeless end was a state of non-existence. The sum of his teaching may be thus expressed:

> Know that, whatever thou hast been,
> 'Tis something better not to be.

To Buddha the highest life was in seclusion, the renunciation of the common duties of home, society, and state. Buddhism makes "celibacy the loftiest state and mendicancy the highest

BUDDHA

idea of life." It has little provision for the great organic institutions of society. The striking contrast between the spirit of Buddhism and Christianity has been sharply drawn by the scholarly Bishop of Ripon: "While Buddha cries 'Retire,' Christ cries 'Advance.' While Buddha cries 'Reduce the powers of affection and happiness,' Christ bids us live fully, enlarging our capacities, strengthening while elevating our affections. The end which Buddha points to is the cessation of suffering; the end which Christ proposes is the perfection of character." Now out of this religion of despair, this petrified pessimism, what may we expect but a man of degraded spirit, without high purpose or lofty ambition or daring enterprise or aggressive courage? And history has not disappointed the dreary expectation. Look at China, a land of heavy slumber and darkness, for which there can be no awakening until it is proclaimed by Christianity's mighty angel of resurrection. From Confucianism we have an impoverished personality. Confucius said he was "a transmitter, not a maker." He taught that religion was reflection. He opposed progress. He abhorred everything new as untrue. He taught nothing with regard to man's relation to God. He said: "The part of wisdom is to attend carefully to our duties to men, and, while we respect the gods, to keep aloof from them." The cardinal doctrine of his creed was the worship of ancestors. Now, from such lifeless, spiritless philosophy and religion we can only expect an impoverished manhood. It has nothing on which to develop stalwart virtues and imperial manliness, nothing to stimulate noble aspiration or to satisfy the divine hunger of the deathless soul. These doctrines, transmuted into the thought and life of the Chinese people, have sterilized the whole nation, and reduced that naturally great power into the plaything and spoil of other governments.

Buddha and Confucianism Degrade Society

The combined influence of Buddhism and Confucianism has produced the civilization of China. It has been compared to Lot's wife, a hardened, stiffened figure, with its face ever toward the changeless past. China sits forever by the grave. Her only ambition is to emulate the dead, her holiest worship is to dwell among the tombs. No wonder she is stationary. There is no future but the past. Departure from old customs is a national crime, variance from the ways of the sages an unpardonable sin. A true picture of this vast nation is a figure sitting before the tablets of the dead; a giant of massive mold and immense capabilities, but a paralyzed and impoverished personality.

The contribution of Hinduism to society is a degraded personality. This is the necessary product of the caste system, which is the distinguishing feature of the Hindu faith. It suppresses the development of individuality and independence of character. Administered as it is with Draconian severity, it brutalizes the conscience and destroys all moral distinctions. A man may commit murder and not lose caste, but receiving a glass of water from the hands of a European would be a mortal sin, the forfeiture forever of all social distinction or recognition. It eradicates human sympathy,

INDIAN WASHERMEN
OF THE LOWER CASTE

annihilates compassion, hardens the heart, and intensifies selfishness. Outside the caste the weal or woe of a fellow-man makes no impression, excites not the least concern. Pity for the low caste is unknown, and measures for their relief would be a contamination. No wonder a distinguished Parsee scholar, while contemplating the degraded and hopeless condition of the Pariah outcasts, exclaimed: "O Caste, thou inexorable tyrant, what hope is there for India while thy Juggernaut wheel is grinding man's best nature out of him?"

Under this system there can be no social unity, no national sentiment, no espirit de corps, no cohesive power. Caste has developed social tyranny and erected family and personal barriers that have necessarily weakened the state. No wonder, therefore, that the great Indo-Aryan race has become the easy prey of invading nations. Buckle, in his *History of Civilization*, has in these graphic words given a faithful picture of that land cursed by caste: "It is not surprising that, from the earliest period to which our knowledge of India extends, an immense majority of the people, pinched by the most galling poverty, and just living from hand to mouth, should always have remained in a state of stupid debasement, broken by incessant misfortune, crouching before their superiors in abject submission, and only fit either to be slaves themselves or to be led to battle to make slaves of others."

And, in addition to this cruel caste, the hideous idolatries of Hinduism can only produce a debased and debauched manhood. No people can rise higher than their conceptions of the gods they worship. Debased deities make degraded votaries. Look at some of those horrid figures before which the superstitious Hindu slavishly bows. There is the stone image of Vishnu, with four arms, riding on a creature half bird, half man, or else sleeping on a serpent. There is Siva, a monster with three eyes, riding naked on a bull, with necklace of skulls for an ornament. There is Kartekeya, the god of war, with six faces, riding on a peacock, and holding bow and arrow in his hands. There is Ganesa, god of success, with four hands and an elephant's head, sitting on a rat. There is Goddess Kali, with flowing

KALI,
A HINDU GOD

hair reaching to her feet, with a necklace of human heads, her tongue protruded from her mouth, and her girdle stained with blood. Before such forbidding creatures, with elaborate and horrid rites of worship, it is impossible for the soul to have pure and noble aspirations. The product of Hinduism can only be a degraded personality. India's sad story has been told by Matthew Arnold in these despairing lines:

> On that hard pagan world, disgust
>> And secret loathing fell,
> Deep weariness and sated lust
>> Made human life a hell.

Christianity and the Three Fold Influence

Now, in contrast with this degrading system, the ennobling virtues of the Christian religion are thus described by a distinguished native of India, a Parsee scholar: "On the other hand, one need not be a Christian himself to be able

to see that Christianity has tended powerfully to humanize one of the least human of the races of men. In its essence it ought to exercise a threefold influence: to humanize, to liberalize, to equalize. This, to me, is a very great achievement. Other religions have their special merits, but none of them claims to have rendered this threefold service to the race."

A KADI, A TURKISH JUDGE

Mohammedanism has produced an enslaved personality. "Its Koran demands intellectual slavery; its harem requires domestic slavery; its state implies and enforces both a religious and a

THE KORAN IN LATIN AND ARABIC

civil slavery." The Koran puts a premium upon war, offering
the highest rewards to those who slay the greatest number
of infidels. Mohammed's cardinal principle, that the end
justifies the means, consecrated every form of deception and
lying, and encouraged every sort of persecution and violence;
commercial confidence is almost unknown, and hence
there are few banks and business partnerships. The citizen
is the slave of the state; he has no rights to be respected.
Mohammedanism is an absolute despotism, the most gigantic
engine of intolerance and persecution the world ever saw.
There is a proverb which says: "Where the Turkish horse
sets its hoof the grass never grows." The Turkish horse is the
synonym of the Turkish government, which is the political
expression of the Moslem religion. In every land swept by
this heartless despotism it has left a tale and trail of blood.
Its simple touch is a blight. Commerce languishes, then
decays; harvests cease, and then the fields become barren as

the uncovered rocks of the eternal hills. All history attests the atrocious verity. A glance at Mohammedan nations will recall the facts of this mournful story. But, while the shrieks of dying Christians in Armenia still linger in our ears—dying by the cruel edge of the Turkish swords, wielded by Turkish slaves, and in order to propagate the Moslem faith—we may well veil from our eyes the desolations of Mohammedan generations.

By the side of these developments of character let us place the Christian conception of manhood. The dignity and individuality of man, with personal, inalienable rights, and entitled to the largest freedom consistent with the rights of others, is the "exclusive legacy of Christianity to humanity." In no land untouched by the Christian religion has such a conception ever obtained. The doctrine of equality of citizenship—equality in privilege unaffected by possession or position—is only another form of our Lord's declaration that "A man's life consisteth not in the abundance of the things which he possesseth." Every human soul has an intrinsic value. Christianity alone has heard and answered the anxious prayer of humanity, voiced in these lines:

> O Freedom, deepen thou a grave,
>   Where every king and every slave
> Shall drop in crown and chain,
>   Till only man remain.

And Christ has brought to the world the blessed doctrine of the brotherhood of man—a brotherhood that "involves an equality of right on the one hand, and a sovereignty of duty on the other." Belief in many gods is irreconcilable with the doctrine of a common humanity. Max Muller tells us

that the word "mankind" never fell from the lips of Socrates
or Plato or Aristotle. "Where the Greeks saw
barbarians, we see brethren; where the Greek
saw nations, we see mankind."

SOCRATES

Christianity and Humanity

After a critical examination of the influence
of the Roman empire in promoting national
unity, Von Humboldt said:

PLATO

> But the feeling of communion and
> unity of the whole human race, and of the
> equal rights of all its families, is derived
> from a nobler source. It is founded upon
> deeper motives of the mind, and upon

ARISTOTLE

> religious convictions.
> Christianity has assisted
> most powerfully in promoting the
> idea of the human race: it has acted
> beneficially in rendering man more
> human in his manners and institutions.
> The idea of humanity is interwoven with
> the earliest Christian doctrines.

WILHELM VON
HUMBOLDT

Christianity and Women in Civilization

Religions, as social and political factors, are also differentiated
by their influence upon the family. A religion that fails to purify
the home is powerless to elevate the nation. The corner-stone

of the commonwealth is the hearthstone. The state is but the enlargement of the family; or, as Prof. Woodrow Wilson happily phrases it, "State is family writ large." And as woman is head of the home, a nation is no better than its women. If

WOODROW
WILSON

they are ignorant and depraved, the family will be impure and the nation debauched. In all non-Christian lands there are no *homes*, only houses. Women are looked upon as slaves or animals. The family life is debauched. The harem is the scene of bitter jealousies, fierce hostilities, and nameless debaucheries. A missionary once asked a Modammedan woman how she felt when a second wife came into the house. She smote upon her breast and said: *"Fire here—fire in the heart."* Out of such houses of shame and sorrow can not be developed the virtues that construct great nations and give glory to empires. For those schools of national character we must look to Christianity, which seeks to make every home as sacred as the shrine of a temple and every woman as pure as the bride of Christ.

In his great work on the *Divine Origin of Christianity, Indicated by Its Historical Effects*,[1] Dr. Storrs thus eloquently refers to woman's indebtedness to the ennobling influences of the Christian religion: "The tendency of Christianity always has been, while recognizing the sex in souls, to give to woman larger opportunity, more effective control of all instruments for work: to put her side by side with man in front of all the great achievements–in letters, arts, humanities, missions–as at the majestic south portal of Strasburg cathedral the figure of Sabina, maiden and architect, faces the figure of Erwin von Steinbach; and though the old traditions of law are hard to change, the entire movement of modern society is toward the perfect enfranchisement of the sex to which the religion brought by Jesus gave at the outset preeminent honor."

Christianity and International Relations

Christianity has also given the world a *new law of international comity,* and has brought the nations of earth into closer fellowship. The historian Lecky has well said: "Christianity has never been an enemy to national feeling, though she has infused into Christendom a bond of unity which is superior to the divisions of manhood." The great and beneficent fabric of *international law* is the direct product of the Christian religion. It comes from the doctrine of universal brotherhood: that all nationalities, however distant and divergent, are members of a higher spiritual family, and that as the spirit of kinship is enthroned the possibility of wars and blood will be reduced. Edward Everett paid this generous tribute to our holy religion in his review of the great work by Grotius: "The foundations of his immortal treatise on the law of nations

HUGO GROTIUS

are laid in the scriptures of the Old and New Testaments, and the original conception of the work was in the genuine spirit of Christian philanthropy."

And its mission of peace on earth and good will to men

continues with increasing success. It has introduced the doctrine of arbitration for the settlement of international controversies, and is daily decreasing the occasions for strife. If it has not yet made wars to cease on the earth, it has greatly mitigated their barbarities, and some day will usher in that cloudless morning which Alfred Tennyson saw in a vision, when

> The war-drums will throb no longer,
>   and the battle-flags be furled,
>   in the parliament of man,
>   the federation of the world.

Protestantism vs. Romanism in Culture

This study might be profitably extended into a *comparison of Protestantism and Romanism,* in their effects upon the civilization of the world. Not all so-called Christian nations are alike. They are separated widely, radically, sometimes fatally. The distinguishing doctrines of Christianity may be variously interpreted, and held with different degrees of spiritual intelligence and moral honesty. So Christian nations differ from each other, not so much from climatic and traditional reasons, but because of variant and even divergent conceptions of the cardinal principles of Christianity. These differences are not attributable to race, climate, or nationality. The cleavage is along the line of religion. Sons of the same blood, heirs of the same promise, have built different civilizations under the same sun and on the same soil. All history attests the truth of Lord Macaulay's eloquent words: "Whoever passes in Germany from a Roman Catholic to a

Protestant principality, in Switzerland from a Roman Catholic to a Protestant canton, in Ireland from a Roman Catholic to a Protestant county, finds that he has passed from a lower to a higher grade of civilization. On the other side of the Atlantic the same law prevails. The Protestants of the United States have left far behind them the Roman Catholics of Mexico, Peru, and Brazil. The Roman Catholics of Lower Canada remain inert, while the whole continent around them is in a ferment with Protestant activity and enterprise."

But the limits of this lecture will not allow a more extended comparison. The story of one country is substantially the history of all others. Romanism sterilizes; Protestantism vitalizes. The one is adapted to a feudal state; the other creates a free commonwealth.

And now the sum of all this discussion is eloquently stated by Wendell Phillips in these words: "The answer to the Shasters is India; the answer to the Koran is Turkey; the answer to the Bible is the Christian civilization of Protestant Europe and America." To which Rev. Dr. W.J.R. Taylor very properly offers this important amendment: "The answer to Romanism is Spain and Mexico; and the answer to atheism is the Reign of Terror in France and the Commune in Paris."

Notes

1. Richard S. Storrs, *Divine Origin of Christianity, Indicated by Its Historical Effects* (New York: Anson D.F. Randolf & Co., 1884).

CHAPTER 2

The Christian Coming and Character of the Early Colonists

THE GENERAL PRINCIPLES discussed in the first chapter—the influences of religion upon civil government—must now be applied to the colonial period of American history. We will ascertain, if possible, how far those great basal principles find illustration and verification in an analysis of the formative forces of our vast republic. From broad generalizations we proceed to historic application.

In the former chapter it was sought to be shown that religion was the determining and dominant factor in all civilizations, and, therefore, the purer the religion the higher the civilization and the wiser the civil government. In illustration of this doctrine the civilizations of Christian and non-Christian countries were contrasted, resulting in the triumphant vindication of Christianity as the mightiest political influence and social dynamic known to the history of the world. Comparison was also instituted between Protestantism and Romanism as civilizing and national forces, revealing the fact that our Protestant faith is the social hope of the world, the only true friend of freedom, the only

IN 1620, A SMALL BAND OF ENGLISH SEPARATISTS
SET SAIL FOR THE NEW WORLD

redeemer of nations, the only palladium of civil liberty, the only wise master-builder of permanent empires.

Colonized by Protestants

It ought, therefore, to be an occasion of unceasing gratitude to every American patriot that this mighty continent was colonized by Protestant England rather than by Catholic France and Spain; that the early rulers of America were the sturdy sons of a pure Protestantism and not the fanatical votaries of an effete Romanism. When Columbus, steering west, and nearing the shores of an undiscovered world, saw a flock of landbirds toward the south, he changed his course to follow their flight, and gave to Spain the West Indies Islands. But for those winged messengers of the wilderness, guided, it may be, by a favoring Providence, the great voyager would have come directly to the shores of Carolina, and this magnificent country, so distinctly Protestant and powerful, might have become the sterile land of an unprogressive Catholic civilization. Instead of a vigorous, aggressive nation, this might have been another pitiable South American republic, scourged with poverty and treachery. Instead of the home of Magna Charta, it might

FIRST SIGHTING OF LAND

have been the land of the guillotine and the Inquisition.

It is a suggestive fact that the first bloodshed in America by Europeans was prompted by Roman Catholic fanaticism. The ferocious assassins who led in the massacre were accompanied by twelve Franciscans and four Jesuits, who gave them the benedictions of the Church. A company of humble, brave-hearted Huguenots fled from persecution in France, and, crossing the Atlantic, formed

HUGUENOTS LAND AT NEW ROCHELLE

ST. BARTHOLOMEW'S DAY MASSACRE, 1572

a little colony near the mouth of the St. Johns River, in Florida. But the presence of these harmless heretics excited Spanish alarm and hate, so the next year (1565) an expedition was fitted out under the command of the distinguished Pedro Melendez, "a bigot, who could conceive of no better manifestation of love to God than cruelty to man, when man was heretical." The helpless colony was cruelly invaded and all swung to the trees, with this inscription written underneath: "Hung as heretics, and not as Frenchmen." So America's first tragedy was a new St. Bartholomew's day, the heartless expression of Catholic casuistry and cruelty. Well would it have been for Spain in that early time if she had been able to hear and heed the philosophic and wise counsel of some leader like her own Emilio Castellar of today. "National freedom," says this Spanish statesman, "can be won only by pacific means. Soldiers are as unfit to build the temple of freedom as the warrior David was to build the temple of God. Those who depend upon the sword shall perish by the sword."

Had the early colonists of America come from other lands, impelled by other motives and inspired by another religious faith, the results would have been vastly different. The brilliant history of the American commonwealth could never have been written. The grand doctrines that have been wrought into the vast framework of this great republic were incarnated in the colonists. Their everlasting principles have become our magnificent institutions. "Our nation, in its greatness to-day, is nothing more than the oak which has sprung from the acorn which they planted." Such a nation could only have been born of a sturdy Protestant faith. The Declaration of Independence could never have been penned by a man, or adopted by a people who accepted the doctrines and were dominated by the principles of a papal hierarchy. It has a Protestant inspiration. But these and other great historic facts will be clearly developed in the process of this discussion.

POPE LEO X

I invite you in this lecture to a study of the *early colonists, their motives, character, and principles.* For the magnificent history of our country we are indebted more than anything else to what the eloquent Sergeant S. Prentiss called the *"awful virtues of our pilgrim sires."* We will therefore most reverently inquire who they were, *what* principles they embraced and taught, and *whither* and *when* and *why* they came. It will be found, I doubt not, that *religion* was the controlling motive of their coming and the divine purpose of their remaining. "With this," as Bancroft says, "the wounds of the outcast were healed and the tears of the exile sweetened."

Avarice and Religious Zeal

Indeed, long before the days of permanent colonization we find this ardent religious purpose directing all westward movements. It characterized and largely controlled the period of discovery. It was alike regnant in Catholic and Protestant. Sails were set in the name of the cross as well as the crown, and lands were claimed both for the Church and the king. But in asserting that religion was the primary motive of American discovery, I do not overlook or undervalue other determining forces. Maritime enterprise, commercial greed, political ambition, and territorial expansion exercised the full measure of their power in speeding the ships that swept the Western seas in search of unseen continents. "Avarice and religious zeal were singularly blended."

THE BOY COLUMBUS

In the national art gallery of Mexico there is a magnificent portrait of Christopher Columbus. He is a young man, with the pale face of a student, and wearing an expression of seriousness deepening to sadness, as though in his heart some long-unrequited hope were about to die. He is sitting on a rock that juts out into sea, and is peering thoughtfully over the restless waves, while maps and charts are spread out before him, and in one hand is a much-used compass. Before that busy brain visions of far-off unknown lands had already passed, and upon that burdened young soul had been rolled the holy mission of their discovery. The sadness that shadowed his fair brow came from the inadequate means at command to fulfil the sublime prophecies of his great soul. That picture, the work of a master, fitly represents the

THE LANDING OF COLUMBUS

scientific and spiritual beginning of this great Western empire.

Columbus was a man of deep piety, and considered himself the "called of God." He felt, as his name, *"Christopher"* implied,

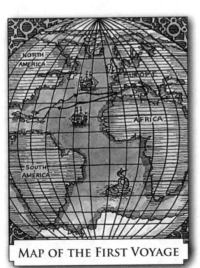

MAP OF THE FIRST VOYAGE

that in an important sense he was a "Christ-bearer." On one occasion he said: "God made me a messenger of the new heavens and the new earth." To his reverent mind his voyage of discovery was little less than a missionary journey. His last act in the Old World and his first in the New were solemn acts of worship. The last note in the Old was a prayer, the first in the New a song. Before launching out to sea the holy communion was celebrated in a temporary chapel at Palos, and so soon as they landed on the island which the great discoverer himself named San Salvador,

SIR HUMPHREY
GILBERT

a cross was erected, and the *Gloria in Excelsis* was sung with loud voice, waking with its swelling cadences the deep silence of a wilderness soon to become a new world.

On his second voyage Columbus was accompanied by twelve priests and a vicar apostolic, with a solemn charge from Queen Isabella to give special spiritual attention to the natives. Other expeditions rapidly followed, each under immediate ecclesiastical benediction and patronage and armed with papal authority to take possession of new countries in the name of "the Church, the queen and sovereign of the world." By the pope's "bull of partition," loyal Catholic nations were to parcel out and possess the New World.

And a like missionary purpose dominated, more or less, the daring enterprise of English voyagers. Sir Humphrey Gilbert, a favorite at the court of Queen Elizabeth, who led several expeditions over the seas, claimed to be filled "with nobler aims than finding ore of gold." His chief ambition, he declared, was "the honor of God, the compassion of poor infidels captivated by the devil," and to "discover all such heathen lands as were not actually possessed by any Christian

CAPTAIN JOHN SMITH

prince or people." And the same announced purpose entered more or less into the daring and ambitious plans of Capt. John

Smith, Sir Walter Raleigh, and other adventurous sailors over the, as yet, uncharted ocean.

But before discussing the period of permanent colonization I pause for a moment to consider a historic fact which has been called a "prodigy of Divine Providence." The *when* of the coming of the colonists is not less significant than the *whither* and the *why.*

The providential planting of the American nation is most manifest in the *time* appointed for the movement to begin. An earlier or a later date would have written for us a different history. "The hour of American colonization was the fittest one, in all modern times, for the New World to receive the best which the Old World had to give." It had a connection in *time* and *spirit* with the Reformation that was more than a fortunate coincidence; it must have been a special and wise providence. For, as the great Dr. Dorner has reverently observed, "a new land arose out of the sea to serve as a bulwark and a reserve for the Church of the Reformation." And on the other hand, God seems to have restrained the spirit of western migration until the forces of the Reformation had wrought a spiritual and political revolution in Europe, and had become sufficiently strong to lay the foundations of a new empire on the other side the seas. "That was high strategy in the warfare for the advancement of the kingdom of God in the earth."

When Columbus touched the shores of San Salvador Luther was a child only nine years old. All Europe was yet under

SIR WALTER RALEIGH

ecclesiastical and civil bondage to the Church of Rome. The papacy was still supreme in Church and State. True, the forces of revolt were slowly forming, but they were waiting for a leader. The dying voice of John Huss was echoing over the continent. Across the channel, Wyclif's English Bible was gradually working the overthrow of ecclesiastical and political despotism. His scattered ashes only symbolized the triumphant

JOHN HUSS

spread of the doctrines he so fearlessly preached in life. Thus a way was being prepared for another "prophet unto the nations," and in the fulness of time he came. The child grew to stalwart manhood, and the humble monk became the intrepid and masterful leader of a movement that had "centuries in its history." From a cloister came this divinely accredited apostle, an open Bible in his hand, girded with power, and armed with pen of fire and tongue of flame. He stirred to its stillest depths the slumbering conscience of nations. His words were battalions, and his doctrines mightier than disciplined armies. Soon every iron crown became uneasy, and almost every throne began to totter. And so it came to pass that "the entire sixteenth century was a period of universal disturbance."

I am sure Guizot limited too narrowly the tremendous results of the Reformation when he asserted that it had little effect politically, but that it "abolished and disarmed the spiritual power, the systematic and formidable government of thought." It was more than an emancipation of mind; it was a political, a national, and international revolution. It was the birth of a new and holier patriotism, the beginning of a larger and freer national life. From it came a broader conception and a bolder assertion of popular rights. Liberty became the world's watchword. The old fable of the divine right of kings began to give way to constitutional governments.

The Reformation wrought the emancipation and exaltation of the State. It abolished the false distinction between the sacred and the secular, and invested magistrates with responsibilities and functions as sacred as those of priest or apostle. An early reformer insisted that "the distinction between ecclesiastical and profane laws can find no place among Christians." They were not to have two consciences, one for the State and another for the Church, but were to be alike loyal to a divine integrity in discharging both the high functions of citizens and churchmen. The Reformation brought the principle of religious liberty "from the region of

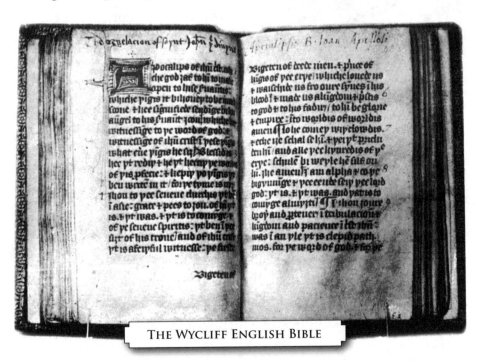

THE WYCLIFF ENGLISH BIBLE

abstract speculation, in which it had been born, into the field of practical politics, where it had no existence."

French and Spanish Influence in North America

MANY OF THE EARLY FRENCH SETTLERS WERE FUR TRADERS

The colonization of North America, whether enterprised by Protestant England or Catholic France and Spain, was more of a religious inspiration than a commercial ambition, a scheme of spiritual propagandism rather than of territorial aggrandizement. Many motives doubtless prompted the coming of the colonists, but the greatest of them all was religious. The earliest in the field were the Spanish and the French. Though strangely restrained by conditions at home, they did push their American conquests with much courage and religious zeal. In the South and on the Pacific coast the Spanish planted themselves, and advanced far into the interior. The French settled along the St. Lawrence, and sought to fortify stations down the entire length of the Mississippi Valley. And everywhere they were guided and commanded by the authority of the Church. The king of Spain said: "The conversion of the Indians is the principal foundation of the conquest." The French advanced their schemes of colonization and conquest, chanting the hymn,

The banners of heaven's King advance;
The mystery of the cross shines forth.

Bancroft says: "It was neither commercial enterprise nor royal ambition which carried the power of France into the

CARDINAL RICHELIEU

heart of our continent: the motive was religion. Religious enthusiasm colonized New England, and religious enthusiasm founded Montreal, made a conquest of the wilderness on the upper lakes, and explored the Mississippi." In all the French and Spanish possessions "not a cape was turned nor a river entered but a Jesuit led the way." Cardinal Richelieu issued the decree that "everybody settling in New France must be a Catholic."

But all those magnificent schemes of empire were doomed to humiliating failure and almost utter extinction. Like a dream as one awaketh, the splendid

THE SPANISH AT TAMPA BAY, FLORIDA, 1539

vision faded away. Only a few somber monuments of French and Spanish dominion remain to remind us of America's providential escape from the iron grasp of a medieval civilization. The issue was finally settled —an issue involving the fate of this continent—on the stormy heights of Abraham. The fall of Quebec was the rise of the American republic. The defeat of Montcalm was the triumph of personal and civil liberty, of the habeas corpus and free inquiry. The victory of Wolfe was the overthrow of civil and ecclesiastical despotism. And so "this echo of the middle ages" passed away.

The Virginia Colony

It was religion that also promoted the colonial settlements established by the sturdy and liberty-loving Protestants. The Virginia colony, the first established by the English in North America, was an avowed measure of religious propagandism. The first charter prescribed their mode of worship, and, in the royal instructions given, the adventurous colonists were "to

VIRGINIA CHARTERS.

NUMBER I.

King JAMES I.'s LETTERS PATENT to Sir Thomas Gates, Sir George Somers, and others, for two several Colonies and Plantations, to be made in VIRGINIA, and other Parts and Territories of AMERICA. Dated April 10, 1606.

I. JAMES, by the grace of God, King of England, Scotland, France, and Ireland, Defender of the Faith, &c. Whereas our loving and well disposed subjects, Sir Thomas Gates, and Sir George Somers, Knights, Richard Hackluit, Clerk, Prebendary of Westminster, and Edward-Maria Wingfield, Thomas Hanham, and Ralegh Gilbert, Esqrs. William Parker and George Popham, Gentlemen, and divers others of our loving subjects, have been humble suitors unto us, that We would vouchsafe unto them

and may in time bring the infidels and savages, living in those parts, to human civility, and to a settled and quiet government ; Do, by these our letters patents, graciously accept of, and agree to, their humble and well intended desires.

IV. And do therefore, for Us, our heirs and successors, Grant and agree, that the said Sir Thomas Gates, Sir George Somers, Richard Hackluit, and Edward-Maria Wingfield, adventurers of and for our city of London, and all such others, as are, or

THE CHARTER OF 1606

provide that the true word and service of God be preached, planted, and used, not only in the said colony but also as much as might be among the savages bordering upon them, according to the rites and doctrines of the Church of England." And one of the chartered reasons assigned for the Jamestown grant was that the colony, "under the providence of Almighty God, might tend to the glory of his Divine Majesty in propagating the Christian religion to such

IDLE COLONISTS IN JAMESTOWN

people as yet live in darkness and miserable ignorance of the true knowledge and worship of God." The first house built after their arrival was a place of worship. Their first penal laws were adopted, as was declared, "to aid the colonists in keeping a good conscience." And when Sir Thomas Dale, the new governor, arrived in 1611, he came furnished with a body of "laws, divine, moral, and martial." When the first legislative assembly met, in 1619, the Church was established by law, and it was enacted that the yearly salary each clergyman should receive from his parishioners was fifteen hundred pounds of tobacco and sixteen barrels of corn, estimated to be worth about two hundred pounds. Each male inhabitant over sixteen years of age was taxed, for this purpose, ten pounds of tobacco and one bushel of corn. In 1624 the colonial assembly further enacted that on every plantation "a house or room" shall be provided for public worship, and attendance upon church service was made compulsory. Thus we see how a fervent religious purpose determined the establishment of the Virginia colony. Of the politico-ecclesiastical questions involved in this and other colonial settlements much will be said in a later discussion.

The Plymouth Colony

The Plymouth colony, which landed thirteen years after the Jamestown settlement, was projected in order better "to practise the positive part of Church reformation and propagate the gospel in America." No devout souls ever made more honest spiritual preparation for the holy worship of the sanctuary than did these noble pilgrims prayerfully perfect their plans to establish a home and new empire in this western wilderness. A solemn fast was observed, then the holy communion was celebrated, and, after a farewell address from the apostolic pastor, Rev. John Robinson, the "Mayflower"

BEGINNING OF NEW ENGLAND

turned her prow toward these far-off shores. With prosperous winds and the guiding Eye which is above storm and billow, the little vessel in due time hailed the heights where in the name of God a new banner was unfurled under the open heavens.

In the cabin of the "Mayflower," anchored off Cape Cod, the Plymouth colonists gathered solemnly around a table, drew up a "compact," and organized themselves into "a civil body politic." This was signed by all the male heads of families and the unmarried men not

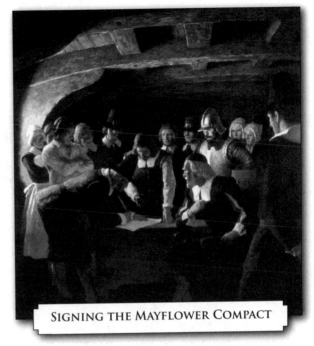

SIGNING THE MAYFLOWER COMPACT

attached to families thus represented. That historic document reads as follows:

> In the name of God, Amen. We whose names are underwritten, the loyal subjects of our dread sovereign lord, King James, by the grace of God, of Great Britain, France, and Ireland, King, Defender of the Faith, etc., having undertaken, for the glory of God and advancement of the Christian faith and honor of our king and country, a voyage to plant the first colony in the northern parts of Virginia, do, by these presents, solemnly and mutually, in the presence of God and of one another, covenant and bind ourselves together into a civil body politic, for our better ordering and preservation, and furtherance of the ends aforesaid, and by virtue hereof to enact, constitute, and frame such just

and equal laws, ordinances, acts, constitutions, and offices, from time to time, as shall be thought most meet and convenient for the general good of the colony: unto which we promise all due submission and obedience. In witness whereof we have hereunder subscribed our names, at Cape Cod, the 11th of November, in the year of the reign of our sovereign lord, King James, of England, France, and Ireland the eighteenth, and of Scotland the fifty-fourth, *Anno Domini* 1620.

KING JAMES I

This, by the way, was the first effort of American colonists to frame a constitution, and out of this grew the more elaborate fundamental law on which this mighty nation is so securely built. The dominant purpose, it is seen, was "to advance the Christian faith," and, free from the fierce persecutions which they had suffered so long, to build a nation in which the conscience should be unfettered and the free worship of God guaranteed. The combined missionary and patriot spirit which impelled their coming is thus expressed by the eccentric and eloquent colonial preacher, Cotton Mather:

COTTON MATHER

> In coming to the new continent they were influenced by a double hope: the enlargement of Christ's

kingdom by the conversion of heathen tribes, and the founding of an empire for their own children in which his religion should gloriously prevail.

The Massachusetts Bay Colony

The colony of Massachusetts Bay was projected with the same religious purpose and the same divine ideal. The Plymouth Company, "for the purpose," says Dr. Baird, in his *Religion in America*, "at once of providing an asylum for persons suffering for conscience' sake in the Old World, and of extending the kingdom of Christ in the New," sold a vast belt of land to a number of English gentlemen. That was the origin of the "colony of Massachusetts Bay." John Winthrop, the accomplished young governor of the colony, on the occasion of leaving the shores of England, thus gave expression to the elevated piety of the brave company in a letter to his father:

JOHN WINTHROP

I shall call that my country where I may most glorify God and enjoy the presence of my dearest friends. Therefore herein I submit myself to God's will and yours, and dedicate myself to God and the company with the whole endeavors both of body and of mind.

And, after embarking, Gov. Winthrop and others drew up a humble request for prayer in their behalf, addressed "to the rest of their brethren in the Church of England." Immediately after landing, a day of solemn fasting and prayer was appointed, and was reverently devoted to the worship of God under the wide-spreading trees of the unbroken forest. They felt that "nothing could be really or permanently prosperous without religion." The colonial seat of Massachusetts in 1628 had the device of an Indian, with this motto in his mouth: "Come over and help us."

The Connecticut Colony

The colony of Connecticut was settled in 1623, and upon the very spot where the city of Hartford now stands. "They too," says Dr. Baird, "carried the ark of the Lord with them, and made religion the basis of their institutions." The solemn compact then adopted, and afterward expanded into their constitution, contained the liberal political principles that yet obtain in that commonwealth.

The New Haven colony was founded shortly afterward, with Rev. John Davenport as spiritual teacher. Their first Sabbath was spent in religious worship under an oak-tree,

JOHN DAVENPORT

the faithful pastor preaching on the Saviour's "temptation in the wilderness." After a day of fasting and prayer they laid the foundation of their civil government by covenanting that "all of them would be ordered by the rules which the Scriptures held forth to them."

The Rhode Island Colony

The Rhode Island colony was founded in 1636 by Roger Williams, the apostle of "soul-liberty" and the champion of civil rights. Unrestricted freedom of conscience and opinion was guaranteed. One writer speaks of "the organization of the community on the unheard-of principle of absolute religious liberty combined with perfect civil democracy." In the compact of 1640 that doctrine was reaffirmed in

ROGER WILLIAMS

these words: "We agree, as formerly hath been the liberties of this town, so still, to hold forth liberty of conscience." And a distinguished professor of Brown University says: "To this day the annals of both city and state have remained unsullied by the blot of persecution."

The Maryland Colony

LORD BALTIMORE

The Maryland colony was planted by Lord Baltimore, a Roman Catholic, under whose wise and liberal administration it rapidly and greatly prospered. The earliest law of Maryland provided that "no person within the province, professing to believe in Jesus Christ, shall be in any way troubled, molested, or discountenanced for his or her religion, or in the free exercise thereof." Generous praise has been given the Catholic governor of this American colony for his large religious toleration, and it has been severely contrasted with the proscriptive, intolerant, persecuting spirit of the New England Puritans. But, while detracting nothing from the high character and splendid qualities of the noble governor, it should

LORD BALTIMORE'S INSTRUCTIONS TO THE COLONISTS

be remembered that the liberal charter of the colony was granted by Protestant England.

Religious Liberty: The Foundation of the Colonies

But time would fail me to relate the story of each struggling colony. They were all born of a common purpose, impelled by a common impulse, and sustained by a common hope. Indeed, so prominent and dominant were the religious principles and scruples of the fathers, that Frederick Maurice characterized the colonies as "sect-commonwealths," connected by their religious convictions and peculiarities. What Dr. Baird has so generously said of early New England may be properly applied to all the colonies: "To their religion the New England colonists owed all their best qualities. Even their political freedom they owed to the contest they had waged in England for religious liberty, and in which, long and painful as it was, nothing but their faith could have sustained them. Religion led them to abandon their country rather than submit to a tyranny that threatened to enslave their immortal minds; and made them seek in the New World the freedom of conscience that was denied them in the Old."

The coming of the colonists was hastened by religious persecution. They were refugees for conscience' sake. Indeed, the noted Dr. Increase Mather, in 1695, went so far as to declare that but for the persecutions of Old England there would not have been a New England. The story is a chapter of horrors. When in 1633 Laud was made Archbishop of Canterbury, persecutions became more cruelly systematic and extreme. Every possible indignity was heaped upon the non-conformists. Occasions

INCREASE MATHER

for their humiliation and degradation were made with fiendish inventiveness. He prohibited the importation of small pocket Bibles from Geneva, which had been popular with the people. Laymen by hundreds were excommunicated for not kneeling when they received the communion. He ordered every minister

WILLIAM LAUD

to read from the pulpit a declaration in favor of Sunday sports. The story is told of one courageous spirit who read the declaration, and then the Ten Commandments, after which he said: "You have heard the commands of man and the commands of God. Obey which you please." King James himself said: "I will make them conform, or hurry them out of the land." Persecution became so fierce in England that a distinguished Puritan statesman on the floor of the House of Commons exclaimed: "Danger enlarges itself in so great a measure that nothing but Heaven shields us from despair."

And on the continent the struggle against an unfettered conscience and the pure worship of God gathered strength for a new onset. The revocation of the edict of Nantes inaugurated another reign of terror for the long-suffering Huguenots. Thousands died by fanatical violence, and other thousands fled from their home and country in disguise and under cover of night, seeking an asylum among those who had less religion but more piety and humanity.

While the storm was thus beating in pitiless fury upon these seemingly hopeless but ever-fearless friends of a true religion, the way of escape to America was opened. In that darkest hour of the struggle for constitutional and religious liberty the westward migration began. "Through scenes of gloom and misery," says Bancroft, "the Pilgrims showed the way to an asylum for those who would go to the wilderness for liberty of conscience. Enduring every hardship themselves, they were the servants of posterity, the benefactors of succeeding generations."

KING CHARLES II

John Norton, of Boston, in a letter to the restored King Charles II, tells the pathetic story of one people, which was the history of all:

> Our liberty to walk in the faith of the gospel with all good conscience, according to the order of the gospel,

was the cause of our transporting ourselves, with our wives, our little ones, and our substance, from that pleasant land over the Atlantic Ocean, into this vast wilderness. . . . We could not live without the public worship of God, nor be permitted the public worship without such a yoke of subscription and conformity as we could not consent unto without sin. That we might, therefore, enjoy divine worship free from human mixtures, without offense to God, man, and our consciences, we, with leave, but not without tears, departed from our country, kindred, and fathers' houses, into this Patmos.

The Character of the Early Colonists

I come now to speak somewhat more particularly of the quality and qualifications of the men who laid the foundations of the American Commonwealth. In nothing is the hand of God more distinctly seen than in the *character of the early colonists.* Mighty men they were, of iron nerve and strong hand and unblanched cheek and heart of flame. God needed not reeds shaken by the wind, not men clothed in soft raiment; but heroes of hardihood and lofty courage to be the voice of a new kingdom crying in this Western wilderness. And such were the sons of the mighty who responded to the divine call. Bishop Hurst says: "With some exceptions they were the wheat of the Old World. Unlike many of our recent immigrants, they came to make here their permanent homes. They cut the last ties that bound them to the elder civilization, and entered heart and soul, for life or death, into the struggle of this new and rising land. Besides, they were religious men, swayed by religious principles, who feared God, and him only. They were men of intelligence, far-sighted, who had been trained in the rough discipline of an age that tried men's souls, and they were thus able to lay broad and deep the foundations of a republic whose cornerstones are freedom and law."

The Independents, who had to flee from England and take refuge in Holland, resolved at length to make their permanent home in the New World. Inured to hardships, accustomed to struggles for life and the means to sustain life, inspired with an undaunted courage born of simple faith in God, they were eminently fitted for the perils of pioneers, and to be the brave builders of a new nation in the wilderness. Their heroic and apostolic minister, the Rev. John Robertson, thus spoke affectionately of his flock soon to be dispersed abroad:

> We are well weaned from the delicate milk of the mother country, and inured to the difficulties of a strange country. The people are industrious and frugal. We are knit together as a body in a most sacred covenant of the Lord, of the violation whereof we make great conscience, and by virtue whereof we hold ourselves strictly tied to all care of each other's good, and of the whole. It is not with us as with men whom small things can discourage.

Their rugged virtues and austere morality were needed for those trying times. Only soldiers who could endure hardness were able to brave the dangers of a wilderness life. They were industrious, self-denying, abstemious, and rigidly conscientious. Their convictions were strong and their purposes inflexible. Of the same blood and faith, they had the steady nerve and sustained courage of Cromwell's ironsides. To them the Bible was everything: "the source of religious principles, the basis of civil law, the supreme authority in matters of common life." With the exception of the colony of Lord Baltimore all were Protestants, and, as Dr. Dorchester properly characterizes them, were "men of stern and lofty virtues, invincible energy, and iron wills - the fitting substratum on which to build great states." They brought with them the sublime conviction, afterward so forcefully stated by that great Puritan

JOHN MILTON

teacher and epic poet, John Milton, that "the Bible doth more clearly teach the solid rules of civil government than all the eloquence of Greece and Rome."

And what may we not say of *the Quakers,* and of our heirship in their splendid virtues and simple manner of life? The very name is a synonym for rugged honesty and uncompromising integrity. They were the embodiment of civic righteousness. Their unswerving contention was for equal and perfect political privilege. And for these they would almost go to war. Carlyle's quaint estimate of George Fox may also serve as a fit characterization

GEORGE FOX

of his great disciple and friend, William Penn, who brought to America the divine principles of an ideal civilization. He says:

The most remarkable incident in modern history is not the Diet of Worms, still less the battle of Austerlitz, Waterloo, Peterloo, or any other battle, but George Fox making himself a suit of leather. This man, the first of the Quakers, was one of those in whom the divine idea is pleased to manifest itself and, across all the hills of ignorance, shine in awful and unspeakable beauty. He is a highly accredited prophet of God.

WILLIAM PENN

With a spirit just as heroic, a purpose just as pure, and a courage just as undaunted, William Penn led an expedition to this Western world; and here, with others, planted the seed from which this mighty nation has grown. He came as an apostle of God, with these words upon his lips: "God in Christ has placed a principle in every man to inform him of his duty and to enable him to do it." Thoroughly imbued with the democracy of Christianity—that we are all brothers of one blood in Christ—he even addressed King Charles II, on one occasion, as "Friend Charles." And so he came across the seas as a sort of incarnated Declaration of Independence. An eloquent utterance of his sounds as though it might have been spoken in an aftertime, on the floor of the Continental Congress: "Any government is free when the people are a party to the laws enacted."

In Penn's address, inviting persons to join his colony far over the Atlantic, he used this language, worthy of a broad-minded Christian and far-seeing statesman:

I purpose, for the matters of liberty, that which is extraordinary—to leave myself and successors no power of doing mischief, that the will of one man may not hinder the good of a whole country. It is the great end of government to support power in reverence with the people and to secure the people from abuse of power; for liberty without obedience is confusion, and obedience without liberty is slavery.

The Quakers of New Jersey drew up a solemn compact, in which it is expressly declared: "We put the power in the people." And in their code of "Concessions and Agreements" may be found the germ of the American constitution. And wherever these God-fearing, simple-minded people found a dwelling-place they stood for freedom of conscience and worship and for the largest personal and civil liberty. Against every form of oppression—everything that erected a barrier between brothers and citizens—they protested with the vehemence of profound conviction. Whittier has given the story of a Quaker girl at Salem, condemned to exile, in default of paying a fine

GENERAL VIEW OF SALEM, MASSACHUSETTS

of 10 pounds for not attending the Puritan Church. When the sheriff proposed to the captain of a vessel to take the condemned maiden to the Barbadoes, the poet made the old hero of the sea respond as follows:

> Pile my ship with bars of silver, pack with coins
> of Spanish gold, From keel-piece to deck-plank, the
> roomage of her hold; by the Living God who made me, I
> would rather in your bay sink ship And crew and cargo,
> than bear this child away.

That stern old commander of the waves must have been a spiritual and political son of George Fox and William Penn. Out of such sturdy stuff came the heroes of the revolution and the builders of the republic.

The Influence of the Huguenots

Of the Huguenots, and our national indebtedness to their rich blood, and pure faith, and sustained courage, and mechanical ingenuity, and tireless industry, and habits of economy, I might speak at undue length. They have contributed much that is best and most enduring in our American civilization, and from them have come many of the greatest statesmen and jurists who adorn our country's brilliant annals.

What a history of storm and sorrow had those brave French reformers! From the massacre of St. Bartholomew under Charles IX to the revocation of the edict of Nantes by Louis XIV, they were the objects of suspicion and pitiless persecution by both royal and ecclesiastical despots.

As the stanch advocates of free conscience, free speech, and free worship—of the divine principles of civil and religious liberty—the Huguenots were considered dangerous alike to the monarchy and the papacy.

So the Jesuit cry rang out: "Crush these things out of the religion of *the Huguenots! Crush out the Huguenots themselves!*" For two hundred years not a synod of their Church could be held, but their faith never faltered and their hope never died. In secret they worshiped their Lord, and on the home altar the holy fires of

HUGUENOT CHURCH
LYONS, FRANCE, 16TH CENTURY

sacrifice never ceased to burn. Every private house became a spiritual temple where the law of the Lord was read and expounded. And thus through two weary centuries these pious patriots prayed and waited for a day of deliverance.

But when the final blow came in the revocation of the edict of Nantes, the remnant of blood, probably five hundred thousand, were compelled to flee the country. Many came to the American colonies, and found hospitable welcome. They scattered over New York and the New England section, but "a warmer climate was more inviting to the exiles of Languedoc," and so they went southward into the Carolinas. Thus it was that South Carolina especially became the "home of the Huguenots," those holy and heroic exiles who fled from fagot and fire to find a peaceful place in which to worship God. I know of no more beautiful picture, spiritual and idyllic, than

Bancroft's pathetic description of those early saints on the way to their devout and joyous Sabbath conventicles. A few passages can not be withheld:

> There it was that the Calvinist exiles could celebrate their worship without fear, in the midst of the forests, and mingle the voice of their psalms with the murmur of the winds which sighed among the mighty oaks. Their church was at Charleston. They repaired thither every Sunday from their plantations, which were scattered in all directions on the banks of the Cooper. They could be seen, profiting by the tide, arriving by families in their light canoes, preserving a religious silence which was alone interrupted by the noise of their oars and the hum of that flourishing village which was watered by the confluence of two rivers.

GEORGE BANCROFT

Better citizens no nation ever had than these pious sons of beautiful France. It has been said, to the credit of their rare virtues and pure home life, that very few of their descendants have ever been arraigned for crime before the courts of the country; and Henry Cabot Lodge has affirmed that "in proportion to their numbers, the *Huguenots* produced and gave to the republic more men of ability than any other."

Mrs. Sigourney, in whose veins flowed the finest Huguenot blood, chanted this prayer for her people, in which all America can devoutly join:

On all who bear their name or lineage may their
    mantle rest:
That firmness for the truth, that calm content
With simple pleasures, that unswerving trust in
Trial, adversity, and death, which cast
Such healthful leaven 'mid the elements
That people the New World.

"Your own state of Georgia was colonized," says Dr. Baird, "expressly as an asylum for imprisoned and persecuted Protestants;" and Dr. Bacon says, "No colony of all the thirteen had a more distinctly Christian origin than this." Godly Moravians from Germany, devout Churchmen and pious Puritans from England, brave Highlanders from Scotland, the heroic Salzburgers from their beautiful Alpine homes, and others, found cordial welcome here from "the good Oglethorpe, one of the finest specimens of a Christian gentlemen of the Cavalier school." Of these, probably the most interesting and least known were the Salzburgers, and yet their Georgia colony, Bishop Hurst affirms, furnishes "one of the most remarkable records of a patient, pure, and uncomplaining religious body in the whole history of the Christian Church." They were descended from the Waldenses. Driven from Austria because of their religious faith, they sought refuge in Protestant lands. Invited by the trustees of the Georgia colony, a large number reached these

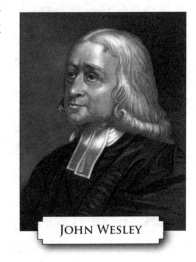

JOHN WESLEY

shores and settled near Savannah. John Wesley found these Salzburgers "among his warmest supporters," and from them Whitefield received generous assistance in building his historic Orphan House. Sturdy, industrious, brave, liberty-loving, their virtues are worthy of all emulation and their names of everlasting honor. One of their favorite hymns is a fair expression of their devout spirit and purpose. What it lacks in poetry is supplied in pathos and piety:

I am a wretched exile here—
Thus must my name be given.
From native land and all that's dear,
For God's word, I am driven.

Full well I know, Lord Jesus Christ,
Thy treatment was no better:
Thy follower I now will be:
To do thy will, I'm debtor.

Henceforth a pilgrim I must be,
In foreign climes must wander:
O Lord, my prayer ascends to thee,
That Thou my path will ponder.

GEORGE WHITEFIELD

But of the coming and character of others I can not, in the limits of this lecture, speak at length. Much should be said of the honest-hearted Hollanders, the founders of New York, who were in advance of all Europe in the struggle for civil liberty, who gave to England herself the first English Bible, the work of Miles Coverdale, printing it at Antwerp, and who for a long period led the world's commerce on the high seas. They imported and reestablished those principles in the New York colony; and on Manhattan Island, which they purchased from the Indians for twenty-four dollars, "built the first free church and the first free school in America."

And then there are the Scotch, who distributed themselves through all the colonies, bringing the simple virtues of their highland homes, preaching the strong gospel of old John Knox, putting honor upon the proper observance of the holy Sabbath, and asserting with dogmatic emphasis the great doctrines of civil freedom. To them we are indebted for the Mecklenberg Declaration of Independence, which was the first ringing of America's liberty-bell. Into the political and spiritual veins of this great nation the rich blood of these and other colonial fathers has been freely poured.

MILES COVERDALE

Such men are God's best gift to a nation, and, as an American divine has eloquently said, "in their grandeur and goodness are worthy to be catalogued with Mount Sinai and with Calvary, for they carry in their personalities and in their feelings and in their principles and in their characters all - all that is contained in the law and the gospel, and all that Sinai and Calvary stand for." By such apostolic and heroic hands our ship of state was built.

> We know what masters laid thy keel,
> What workman wrought thy ribs of steel,
> Who made each mast and sail and rope,

> What anvils rang, what hammers beat
> In what a forge and what a heat
> Were shaped the anchors of thy hope.

For their austere morality the fathers havebeen severely censured and caricatured. The penal codes of the colonial era are now anathematized as cruel even to barbarity, but indiscriminate censure betrays ignorance of historic conditions. We can not judge men of the seventeenth and eighteenth centuries by nineteenth-century ideals and standards. If, however, the colonialists, escaped to the unrestricted freedom of the Western wilderness, are compared with their brothers in England and all Europe, they stand out as reformers of the most advanced and majestic type. Shortly after the "Mayflower" left England the number of offenses punishable with death was thity-one, increased later to two hundred and twenty-three, of which one hundred and seventy-six were without benefit of clergy; while in the American colonies not one recognized more than fifteen capital crimes. So the "dreadful and disgusting inhumanities" of our colonial fathers, so much declaimed against, appear amonth the gentlest amenities, when compared with their kin of the old world.

And there is another view worthy of consideration. The rigidly extreme and sometimes impracticable spirit of the colonists was the normal expression of the things for which they themselves had suffered. That seeming paradox follows an invariable law of the human mind—a fact, by the way, ought to soften all severe criticisms of the early fathers. Whipple, in his *Essays and Reviews*, says: "If a body of men be deprived of their dearest rights for professing conscientious opinions, it is natural that they should attach more importance to those opinions than if they were allowed their free exercise. It not only makes them more sturdy champions of their belief but it leads them into intolerance toward others."

Out of such material institutions of our American commonwealth have been built. And these institutions will abide, because founded on the truth of God, built by faith in the providence of God, and baptized with the blessing of God. Macaulay must for the moment have forgotten or failed to take account of the spiritual element in our political history when he wrote down his gloomy prophecy. "As for America," said he, "I appeal to the twentieth century. Either some Caesar or Napoleon will seize the reins of government with a strong hand, or your republic will be as fearfully plundered and laid waste by barbarians in the twentieth century

BARBARIANS INVADE ROME

as the Roman empire was in the fifth century, with this difference: that the Huns and Vandals who ravaged Rome came from without her borders, while your Huns and Vandals will be engendered within your own country and by your own institutions." In answer to that rather doleful prediction I can not forbear the more optimistic judgment and generous prophecy of a recent and very accomplished historian of England, Prof. John Richard Green:

In the centuries that lie before us the primacy of the world will lie with the English people. English institutions, English speech, English thought, will become the main features of the political, the social, and the intellectual life of mankind.... In the days that are at hand, the main current of that people's history must run along the channel, not of the Thames or the Mersey, but of the Hudson and the Mississippi.

On the rocky summit overlooking the bay where the "Mayflower" first anchored, a magnificent monument has been erected. That colossal statue is at once a miracle, a parable, and a prophecy—a miracle of artistic genius, a parable of Christian civilization, and a prophecy of increasing national glory. On the corners of the pedestal are four figures in a sitting posture—representing Law, Morality, Freedom, and Education. Standing far above, on the lofty shaft of granite, is a majestic figure symbolizing Faith, holding an open Bible in one hand, and, with the other uplifted, pointing far away to the throne of God. What a sublime conception! How true to the facts of our heroic history! That open Bible is the Magna Charta of America, and that uplifted hand, symbolizing trust in the God of our fathers, is the condition of our national stability and continued prosperity.

CHAPTER 3

The Christian Institutions and Laws of the Colonists

IN THE LAST chapter we studied the Christian character of the early colonists, together with the motives that impelled their coming to America, and the pronounced religious principles that dominated their first settlements. It was ascertained that all the earliest schemes of discovery and colonization were inspired by a religious impulse and controlled by a Christian purpose. "We all," says one of the two oldest of American written constitutions, "came into these parts of America to enjoy the liberties of the gospel in purity and peace." Fleeing from ecclesiastical persecution in the Old World, they sought safety in the New, and opportunity to build a nation in which the largest civil and religious liberty, consistent with the rights of others, should be sacredly guarded and guaranteed. To use the words of George Canning, they "turned to the New World to redress the balance of the Old."

GEORGE CANNING

In our analysis of their sturdy characters, we found in them those virile and splendid virtues, out of which all good civilizations are constructed, and which have been so eminently distinctive of the American commonwealth. A noble generation they were. Men who had the spirit of prophecy, the high purpose of an apostolate, and the sublime courage of martyrdom. "We have learned from them," says a distinguished author, "the grand possibilities which wait for men of faith who are content to bow their heads to the storm and commit their way unto the Lord and trust him to bring them to the desired haven."

Our fathers came to these shores as Christians—as Protestant Christians—and on the great cardinal principles of that faith began the making of this nation. Those doctrines "cradled our freedom." We found occasion, therefore, in the process of our investigation, for special thankfulness that this wonderful country was colonized by Protestant England, rather than by Catholic France and Spain. Speaking of the Spaniards, William Cullen Bryant said: "Fortunately for the progress of the human race and the future history of North America, all their efforts to gain a permanent foothold north of the Gulf of Mexico were in the main unsuccessful." And the remark applies with equal force to the colonization plans of all Roman Catholic nations, with their doctrines of a fettered conscience, a sealed Bible, a feudal state, and a medieval civilization. The defeat of Montcalm on the Heights of Abraham was the pivot

WILLIAM CULLEN BRYANT

on which turned the modern history of the world.

In one of the public squares in Boston there is a statue of Gov. John Winthrop, the "Founder of Massachusetts," that devout and able pioneer, who is worthy to be canonized as a saint and chronicled among the statesmen of the world. It is an erect and manly figure, with a Bible in one hand and the charter of the colony in the other. That heroic statue, with the written scroll and the open Book of Heaven, may

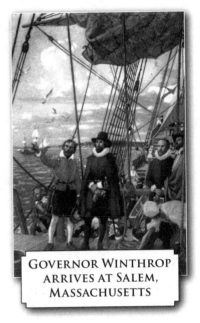

GOVERNOR WINTHROP ARRIVES AT SALEM, MASSACHUSETTS

fittingly represent all the founders of this great republic. By the legal guarantees of the one and the inspired teachings of the other they took possession of this goodly land, and laid the foundations of a Christian nation that has become the marvel and model of modern empires.

Bancroft says that "the colonists from Maine to Carolina— the adventurous companions of Smith, the proscribed Puritans

A QUAKER MEETING

that freighted the fleet of Winthrop, the Quaker outlaws that fled from jails, with a Newgate prisoner as their sovereign—all had faith in God and in the soul." And by that unfaltering faith, more than all else, were they enabled to defy the discouragements and endure the distresses and perils of their wilderness life, while building their heroic principles into the framework of this republic. Whatever is put in a man's religion will express itself in his politics. The governmental doctrines of our fathers, therefore, were the public and political expression of their profound religious convictions.

In this lecture we will proceed with our studies from men to principles—from the character of the colonists to the character of the institutions they established. We will advance from an analysis of the rare virtues of the fathers to an inquiry into the principles embodied in the constitutions they adopted, the laws they enacted, and the social life they created. Thus we will ascertain how far their avowed faiths were crystallized into organic laws, and to what extent they were enthroned in the life of communities. We have a right to expect that men so aggressively religious as to encounter persecution, and so rigidly conscientious as to become exiles rather than submit to ecclesiastical tyranny, would embody their convictions in the government they constructed, and stamp their characters upon the legislation they enacted. Further investigation, I am sure, will not disappoint this well-grounded expectation.

And not only so, but we will have a heightened appreciation for our large and increasing indebtedness to the early colonists. The constitutions under which we live, and the improved educational, industrial, and social conditions of our time, are but the flowering and fruitage from the seeds of their prayerful and patriotic planning. "We are drinking at the fountains which they opened. We walk in their light, and we are to pass on the torch to other generations." Of those mighty champions of liberty, and the idea they developed into our American commonwealth, Longfellow thus sweetly sings:

> God has sifted three kingdoms to find the wheat for
> this planting, then had sifted the wheat, as the living
> seed of a nation.

Those living seed, watched by a favoring Providence,
watered by the tears of a sanctified patriotism, warmed
by the genial sun of civic righteousness, and cultivated by
the industrious hands of a peerless statesmanship, have
produced the magnificent Americanism of to-day. Despite
its defects, and notwithstanding the sad chapters of its
history, our Americanism stands for all that is purest and
grandest in the world's modern civilization. Should any
one ask what has been the contribution of those colonial

THE GIVING OF THE LAW ON MT. SINAI

patriots to civil and religious history, I would answer, in the language of a distinguished historian, as follows:

> Free governments, by the people and for the people; a free press; an enlightened public opinion which controls princes and cabinets; free public-schools,— open to the children of the people; a nobler Christian manhood; a fuller comprehension of the religion of Christ, which brings help and comfort to the poor, which brings liberty to the slaves as those redeemed by the Saviour of the world; the separation of Church and State; the equality of all branches of the Church before the law; freedom within the Church, whether it be prelatical or presbyterian or congregational; a quiet Sunday, with its opportunities for the culture of the spiritual nature; and a free pulpit, in sympathy with all sorts and conditions of men.

Though not realized at once—and at times all hopeful prophecies seemed about to fail—this at last is the harvest of that early sowing.

Motley, the accomplished historian, thus speaks of our great republic:

> The American democracy is the result of all that was great in bygone times. All led up to it. It embodies all. Mount Sinai is in it; Greece is in it; Egypt is in it; Rome is in it; England is in it; all the arts are in it, and all the reformations and all the discoveries.

EXECUTION OF PROTESTANTS IN THE NETHERLANDS BY CHARLES V

That generous judgment is true; but of all the formative forces that have entered into our civic composite life, and given it distinction in modern civilization, the type of Christianity embraced by the fathers was the most potent and permanent. There was a good deal of Mount Sinai in their religion, and it found stern expression in the rigid terms of their early legislation.

The Christianity of the colonists taught the supremacy of conscience, the sovereignty of the individual, the inviolability of private rights, the sacredness of human life, and the brotherhood of man. Out of these cardinal doctrines came the fundamental principles of our republican government: liberty, equality, fraternity, and the protection of life and property. Religious liberty created and sustained an inexorable demand for political liberty. Freedom of conscience claims the right of free speech and personal independence. The facts of history abundantly sustain the statement of Dr. Baird, that "the political institutions of the Puritan colonies of New England are to be traced to their religion, not their religion to their political institutions; and this remark applies to the other colonies also." And the same author states another fact which evidences the religious genesis and genius of the great principles on which this nation is founded. "Persecution," said he, "led the Puritan colonists to examine the great subject of human rights, the nature and just extent of civil government, and the boundaries at which obedience ceases to be a duty."

The religion that holds the conscience of a nation will determine its civilization.

The development of those feeble scattered settlements into solid, self-sustaining colonies, then into independent states, and finally into a powerful union, makes a chapter unique in the annals of empires. Certainly some forces above human control must have been at work. "The history," says Dr. Leonard Woolsey Bacon, "reads like the fulfilment of the apocalyptic imagery of a rock hewn from the mountain without hands, moving on to fill the earth."

But, before entering more in detail upon the study of the character and form of the governments established by the colonial fathers, I wish to make two observations which will be helpful in our investigations and serve as a warning against harsh and hasty conclusions. The one refers to the ecclesiastical and religious intolerance of the colonies, and the other to the severe laws enacted and their inhumane administration. My purpose is not to defend all the acts of the fathers, or approve much of their legislation, but to show that their great desire and high intention were to establish a distinctly Christian commonwealth, in which righteousness should perpetually dwell, and the golden rule of Christ be made the royal law of personal and public life.

Observations on Early Colonial Government

I. Reasons for the Religious Intolerance of the Colonies

It is not surprising that the colonists should have enacted the most rigorous laws against the Roman papacy, and in New England shown the strongest hostility toward the English prelacy. Men whose fathers had been killed by Catholic fanaticism, and whose mothers and sisters had to fly in terror from their homes at night, with scant clothing and not a crust of bread, were not apt to be tolerant toward those who might attain power and repeat such barbarities. John Endicott, cutting out the cross of St. George from the flag of his country, because the cross was a symbol used by the Church of Rome, is not so much a picture of Puritan prejudice as of real fear lest the slightest toleration should lead to the restoration of a despotism that had brutally spilled the blood of his fathers. And the Pilgrims who had been driven from

ENDICOTT CUTTING THE CROSS FROM THE KING'S BANNER

their native land by the Act of Uniformity and the tyranny of the Stuarts would hardly be supposed to look with much favor and hospitality upon the Church of England. Banished from the Old World for not using the *Book of Common Prayer* in public services, they would not be swift to adopt it as their mode of worship in the New. It is a fact not to be wondered at,

TITLE PAGE TO THE *BOOK OF COMMON PRAYER*, 1662

therefore, that "for over sixty years after the Pilgrims landed there was not a single Episcopal church in New England." And as late as 1720, when it was discovered that certain persons connected with Yale College were leaning toward episcopacy, alarm was created "lest the introduction of Episcopal worship into the colony should have a tendency to gradually undermine the foundations of civil and religious liberty." The memories of Archbishop Laud and the Court of Sessions, imprisoning and banishing their fathers, were too vivid and recent for them not to fear a repetition of the same terrible tyranny. In the twelve years from 1628 to 1640 four thousand English families—a total of twenty-one thousand persons—came to these shores "under stress of the tyranny of Charles Stuart and the persecution of William Laud." Indeed, so direful were the cruelties

YALE COLLEGE, NEW HAVEN

that drove nearly all our colonial fathers across the seas, that Bancroft has said: "The history of our colonization is the history of the crimes of Europe."

There was another reason why the colonies of New York

INDIANS ATTACK THE COLONISTS

and New England especially should have shown intolerance toward the Roman Catholics - the incitement by Jesuit missionaries of the Indians to repeated bloody massacres. Their complicity in those scenes of carnage led the New York Assembly in the year 1700 to pass "an act against Jesuits and popish priests," which recited the facts of their seditious conduct. And this necessitated the aggressive action of the government of Massachusetts against the French Jesuit missionary, Father Sebastien Rale. Some papers of his fell into the hands of the government, which furnished conclusive evidence of the fact that he had led an Indian expedition against the English settlers. Such treachery in the name of the Church was quite sufficient to occasion the most vigorous measures of expatriation and protection.

II. RATIONALE BEHIND THE SEVER LAWS

Another fact must be borne in mind as we study the seemingly rigid institutions and harsh legislation of the colonists: *they lived back in the seventeenth century,* and were not exempt from the spirit of that age. They are to be compared, therefore, with seventeenth rather than nineteenth century standards. Measured by that rule, "they were the progressives of their age, and were the most merciful people of that century." Their laws were in milder form and the penalties were less severe than any known to that period of blood and iron. And yet most forbidding pictures have been drawn of the brave and hardy pioneers, as though they were monsters of cruelty and exceptions in all history for the enormity of their inhumanities in the name of religion. The story of burning the witches has been repeated with such pious horror, as though that fanaticism never occurred outside the American colonies. There was intolerance, civil and ecclesiastical, not to be defended, and there were laws enacted and regulations adopted that seem to us in this day exceedingly ludicrous; but we must remember that they lived in the seventeenth century, and that they were the gentlest and best people of their time.

BURNING "WITCHES" IN EUROPE

In this connection I commend the following judicious and accurate statement by an accomplished historian: "No intelligent student of their history will ignore the fact that the world has made marvelous progress since 1620. The belief in witchcraft was, I think, universal in Christendom, in that age.

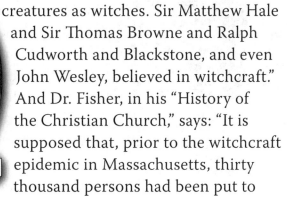

The great jurists and philosophers of England were confident that there were such creatures as witches. Sir Matthew Hale and Sir Thomas Browne and Ralph Cudworth and Blackstone, and even John Wesley, believed in witchcraft." And Dr. Fisher, in his "History of the Christian Church," says: "It is supposed that, prior to the witchcraft epidemic in Massachusetts, thirty thousand persons had been put to death in France, and one hundred thousand in Germany." It related that those deaths in Germany were caused by the bull issued by Pope Innocent the Eighth.

But this outburst of superstition and fright against witchcraft only continued for less than two years, and was arrested by the aroused moral sentiment of the colonists themselves, without suggestion or pressure from abroad. In England and on the Continent it raged for many years thereafter. And it is well also to recall a fact stated in the former lecture, that in not one of the colonies were there more than *fifteen* crimes punishable with death, while in England the number was *thirty-one.*

It may be well also, while considering these exaggerations that have so grossly misrepresented the colonists, to refer to the case of Roger Williams. While detracting nothing from his fearless courage, perfect sincerity, and great conscientiousness, and reiterating the highest appreciation of his valuable contributions to the cause of civil and religious liberty, I must

ROGER WILLIAMS
IN EXILE

believe that his banishment was more attributable to his obstinacy and contentiousness than to the intolerance and inhumanity of his fellow colonists. He declaimed against the charter of the colony as without authority; declared that the people had no title to their lands; taught that it was unlawful to even worship with the unregenerate, though members of one's own family, and that it was unlawful to administer an oath to a citizen who was not a Christian. He was a constitutional separatist. A minister of the Church of England, he left that body to become an Independent, then he became a Baptist by self-appointment in a church of his own organizing, and afterward left that, to die outside the communion of any Christian Church. One historian speaks of Roger Williams as "separating himself not only from the English Church, but from all who would not separate from it, and from all who would not separate from these, until he could no longer, for conscience' sake, hold fellowship with his wife in family prayers." It is a pleasure, however, to know that his sentence of banishment was revoked some years thereafter, when troubles came upon him, and an order was entered that Mr. Williams "shall have liberty to repair into any of our towns for his security and comfortable abode during these public troubles."

The Character and Form of Colonial Government

Probably *the first distinctive act toward representative government in America* was that of the Virginia colony in 1619, a year before the Pilgrims landed at Plymouth Rock. The burgesses assembled in Jamestown, July 30, 1619, and the historic meeting of the little legislature was held in the church. From the contemporaneous account sent to England by the Speaker, I quote as follows:

> The most convenient place we could finde to sitt in was the Quire of the Church, when Sir George Yardley, the Governor, being sett down in his accustomed place, those of the Counsel of Estate sate nexte him on both handes, except only the Secretary, then appointed Speaker, who sate right before him. John Twine, Clerke of the General Assembly, being placed nexte to the Speaker, and Thomas Peirse, the Sergeant, standing at the barre, to be ready for any service the Assembly should command him. But forasmuche as men's affairs doe little prosper where God's service is neglected, all the burgesses took their places in the Quire till a prayer was said by Mr. Bucke, the minister, that it would please God to guide and sanctifie all our proceedings to his owne glory, and the good of this plantation. Prayer being ended, to the intente that as we had begun

RUINS OF OLD
CHURCH, JAMESTOWN

at God Almighty, so we might proceed with awful and due respecte towards the Leiutenant, our most gratious and dread soveraigne, all the Burgesses were intreated to retyre themselves into the body of the Churche, which being done, before they were freely admitted, they were called to order and by name, and so every man (none staggeringe at it) tooke the oath of Supremacy, and then entered the Assembly.

Thus it will be seen that the first movement toward democracy in America was inaugurated in the house of God and with the blessing of the minister of God. And this interesting incident leads to the statement of a momentous fact: that *in America, the state was the outgrowth of the Church.* The sanctuary built the nation. "In all affairs," says Dr. Dorchester, "civil and ecclesiastical, the Church took the precedence, and gave character to the civil administration; the State was only the Church acting in secular and civil affairs." The ballot was restricted to members of the Church. This suffrage law was adopted in 1631, and, however unwise such action may now be considered, we can not but honor the patriotic and religious purpose that inspired it. They desired to lodge political power only in the hands of good men. It was not an ecclesiastical ambition to subordinate State to Church, but a misguided effort, it may be, to save the State from a corrupt and dangerous citizenship. That franchise clause, adopted by the Massachusetts Bay colony, reads as follows:

DANIEL DORCHESTER

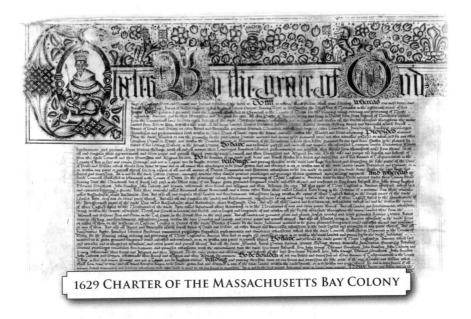

1629 CHARTER OF THE MASSACHUSETTS BAY COLONY

To the end that the body of the Commons may be preserved of honest and good men, no man shall be admitted to the freedom of this body politic but such as are members of some of the Churches within the limits of the same.

This, or a similar statute, was adopted by the colonial government of Maine, Massachusetts, and Connecticut. In Connecticut the law was more liberal: residents of accepted character might be admitted as freeman, but the Governor must be a member of the Church. The New Haven colony restricted the suffrage to Churchmembers, and adopted the Scriptures as the law of the land. And in all the colonies, except Rhode Island and Pennsylvania, ministers of the gospel were supported by public taxation. But in extenuation of such legislation it must be remembered that throughout Christendom at that time it was "the universal prerogative of the Church to confer the civil franchise," and it was the admitted duty of all citizens to support the Church. The whole argument of those devout and heroic colonists has been stated by Dr. Dorchester in a single sentence:

> The key principle was that government, civil and ecclesiastical, is constituted and administered upon the Bible as the source of knowledge and authority.

And this principle controlled in all the laws framed for the government of the colonies. The first general court of the Connecticut colony adopted a set of laws, and prescribed that all deficiencies in the same were to be supplied by the Word of God. Basing their ideas of government upon the ancient Hebrew theocracy, the Massachusetts colony passed this act: "No custom nor prescription shall ever prevail amongst us . . . that can be proved to be morally sinful by the Word of God." The governor of the colony of New York was charged to "take special care that God Almighty be devoutly served throughout the government." In Virginia stringent statutes were enacted for the punishment of blasphemy, to compel observance of the Lord's day, attendance upon public worship, etc.; and one provided that a person denying the existence of God, or the Trinity, or the authority of the Scriptures, should forfeit all official positions within the province.

The chapter of laws adopted by the Quaker colony of Pennsylvania is so curious in phrase and spirit, that I can not refrain from giving a liberal extract:

> Whereas the glory of Almighty God, and ye good of mankind, is the reason and end of government, and therefore government in itself is a venerable

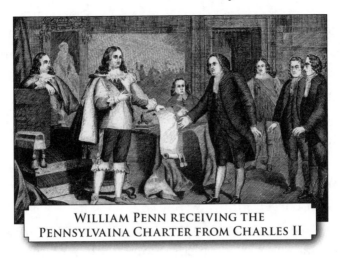

WILLIAM PENN RECEIVING THE
PENNSYLVAINA CHARTER FROM CHARLES II

ordinance of God; and forasmuch as it is principally
desired and intended by the proprietary and governor,
and the freedom of the province of *Pennsylvania,* and
territories thereunto belonging, to make and establish
such laws as shall best preserve true Christians and
civil liberty, in opposition to any unchristian, licentious,
and unjust practises, whereby God may have his due,
Caesar his due, and the people their due, and insolency
and licentiousness on the other, so that the best and
firmest foundation may be laid for the present and
future happiness both of the governor and people of this
province and territorys aforesaid and their posterity:
Be it therefore enacted by William Penn, proprietary
and governor, by and with the advice and consent of the
deputys of the freemen of this province and counties
aforesaid in assembly mett, and by the authority of the
same, that these following chapters and paragraphs shall
be the laws of Pennsylvania and the territorys thereof.

Then, after granting the most liberty of conscience and worship, in order that looseness, irreligion, and atheism might not creep into the body politic, the law provides for the observance of the Sabbath, punishes profane swearing and cursing, and further enacts, that "whoever shall speak loosely and profanely of Almighty God, Christ Jesus, the Holy Spirit, or Scriptures of truth, and is thereof legally convicted, shall forfeit and pay five pounds, and be imprisoned for five days in the house of correction."

Most remarkable indeed were these efforts of the fathers to establish a pure Christian commonwealth. And in many respects they were far in advance of their age. As nation-builders they were republican pioneers.

Dr. Leonard Bacon says:

MOSES AND THE
TEN COMMANDMENTS

The greatest and boldest improvement which has been made in criminal jurisprudence by any one act since the dark ages was that which was made by our fathers when they determined that 'the judicial laws of God, as they were delivered by Moses, and as they are a fence to the moral law, being neither typical nor ceremonial nor having any reference to Canaan, shall be accounted of moral equity, and generally bind all offenders and be a rule to all the courts.'

The pious sturdy colonists brought with them also a sacred regard for the holy Sabbath, and they enacted laws for its rigid observance. Some of these seem rather ludicrous and extreme, but evidence the straightforwardness and sincerity of those heroic men, out of whose sublime virtues this nation has been evolved. Little labor was performed, and scant food was prepared on that solemn day. All the recreation deemed necessary were two long walks, deliberate, silent, and solemn, to and from the house of worship. But that gruesome Sabbath, so much declaimed against, has done much to make glorious the civilization and history of this great republic.

Of the so-called "Connecticut Blue Laws" I need not speak to this audience, for all well-informed persons know that they never existed in fact, but were the malicious fabrication of one Samuel Peters, a Tory and an English clergyman who had been driven from the country on account of his disloyalty during the war of the Revolution.

Some things in their manner of thought and life are certainly very curious, if not ludicrous.

Dr. Dorchester, in his admirable *History of Christianity in the United States*, reproduces an ancient document written in Danvers, Mass., in 1713, which shows the grotesque Sabbath scruples that obtained in that day:

> When the services at ye house were ended, the council and other dignitaries were entertained at the house of Mr. Epes, on the hill near by, and we had a bountiful table, with Bear's meat and venison, the last of which was from a fine Buck shot in the woods near by. The bear was killed in Lynn Woods near Reading. After the blessing was craved by Mr. Garrish, of

Wenthom, word came that the buck was shot on the Lord's day by Pequot, an Indian. Like Anania of old, the council, therefore, refused to eat of the venison, but it was agreed that Pequot should receive forty stripes save one for lying and profaning the Lord's day, restore Mr. Epes the cost of the deer; and considering this a just and righteous sentence on the sinful heathen, and that a blessing had been craved on the meat, the council all partook of it but Mr. Shepard, whose conscience was tender on the point of venison.

The Colonial Meeting House

I invite you next to consider *the influence of the ministry and the "meeting-house" upon colonial institutions.*

"According to the system established in Massachusetts," says Hildreth in his *History of the United States,* "the Church and State were most intimately blended. The magistrates and general court, aided by the advice of the elders, claimed and exercised a supreme control in spiritual as well as temporal matters; while even in matters purely temporal the

BAPTIST MEETING HOUSE
PROVIDENCE, RI

elders were consulted on all important questions." The central building and ruling influence through all the colonial period was the meeting-house. "The village grew up around it, and the country roads were laid out with reference to it." And so permanent and potential has been that influence that James Russell Lowell said: "New England was all meeting-house when I was growing up." It was a sanctuary of worship on the Sabbath, and a hall of legislation and administration during the week. There was held the town meeting, "that little congress of the local democracy which was the germ of the republic," and all its deliberations were opened with an earnest invocation and closed with the apostolic benediction.

The most influential and honored person in every parish was the colonial clergyman. The parson was what his name implied, the chief person in every community. He was consulted not only about questions in morals and theology, but about matters of legislation and civil administration. In some instances he was called upon to prepare important state papers, and to go on delicate and dangerous missions and embassies. Dr. Increase Mather was entrusted with a mission that demanded the most skilful diplomacy, and achieved such success as called forth the highest expressions of praise and gratitude. The Levitical

AARON THE LEVITE
HIGH PRIEST

priesthood, in Jewish history, "constituted," says John Stuart Mill, "the firm vertebral column which secured the historic unity of the nation throughout the changing generations." And another author thus refers to the same suggestive fact: "A bond of union running through the tribes was the tribe of Levi, which were given cities within the territories of other tribes, instead of a territory of their own, so that they might reside in every part of the country, and keep the people in mind of that national covenant which made them one people." This means of spiritual instruction and propagandism was incorporated into the political life and found striking illustration of the American colonies, and was probably the most efficient agency in producing and strengthening the national spirit that ultimately found expression in the majestic union of sovereign states. Some years ago, in one of his Boston Monday lectures, Joseph Cook gave utterance to a similar opinion, but his statement as to Mr. Wesley was inaccurate: "It is sometimes said that Wesley and Whitefield, moving up and down the Atlantic coast as shuttles, wove together the sentiments of the thirteen colonies, and made union possible by creating a national spirit."

Ministers of the colonial period, whether churchmen or dissenters, were men in authority. Their influence was unbounded, determining, as they did, all questions in the colony, "from the choice of a governor to that of the village school teacher." They belonged to an order of democratic nobility. They commanded the profoundest respect of the older, and to the children they were the "most vivid image of respectability and majesty." The minister's "calmly awful" appearance, and his quaint dress and three-cornered hat, form a distinct picture of social life in the second generation of the colonial times. Mrs. Stowe's description of Dr. Samuel Hopkins may serve as a portrait of the ministers of that day, whether churchman in Virginia or Puritan in new England.

He entered the dining-room with all the dignity of a full-bottomed, powdered wig, full flowing coat with ample cuffs, silver knee and shoe buckles, as became the majesty of a minister of those days. The company rose at his entrance. The men bowed, and the women courtesied; and all remained standing while he addressed to each, with punctilious decorum, those inquiries in regard to health and welfare which preface a social interview.

In Massachusetts the magistrates and general court exercised no important function and adopted no unusual measures without "the advice of the elders." And when, in 1649, the first codification of the laws of that colony was made, the commission appointed for the purpose consisted of "two magistrates, two ministers, and two able persons from among the people of each county." Into that code some ancient laws of the Hebrews were literally transferred. The "Body of Liberties" adopted by the colony a few years before was prepared by Rev. Nathaniel Ward of Ipswich, a man learned in law and divinity. "This code," says Bancroft,

THOMAS HOOKER'S EMIGRATION TO CONNECTICUT

"for liberality and comprehensiveness, may vie with any similar record from the days of Magna Charta." At the first session of the general court of the colony of Connecticut, which he had founded, Thomas Hooker preached a sermon in which he said:

> The foundation of authority is laid in the
> free consent of the people; the choice of public
> magistrates belongs unto the people, by God's own
> ordinance; . . . they who have power to appoint
> officers and magistrates have the right to set the
> bounds and limitations of the power and place of
> those who are called.

A striking evidence of the potential influence exercised by the colonial clergy in the administration of civil affairs and their valued contributions to the foundations of our republican government is found in Bancroft's elaborate account of a certain political crisis. It was in 1676, when a serious breach had occurred growing out of the enforcement of the acts of nagivation. The colonists made firm resistance, and determined to fall, if fall they must, with dignity and unstained integrity. And, as was their pious custom, they went to the house of prayer to find grace and wisdom for their political trials. The great historian says: "Religion had been the motive of the settlement; religion was now its counselor. The fervors of the most ardent were kindled; a more than usually solemn form of religious observance was adopted; a synod of all the churches in Massachusetts was convened to inquire into the causes of the dangers to New England liberty and the mode of removing the evils." And thus the early patriots sought counsel from the Most High in determining what was duty in a national crisis.

Among the greatest of colonial patriots was the Rev. Jonathan Mayhew, and out of his religious convictions was born his sublime devotion to the cause of civil freedom and independence. "Instructed in youth," as he said of himself, "in the doctrines of civil liberty, as they were taught by such men as Plato, Demosthenes, Cicero, and others among the ancients; and such as Sidney and Milton, Locke and Hoodly, among the moderns, I liked them; and having learned from the Holy Scriptures that wise, brave, and virtuous men were always friends to liberty, that God gave the Israelites a king in his anger, because they had not sense and virtue enough to like a free commonwealth, and that where the spirit of the Lord is there is liberty, this made me conclude that freedom is a great blessing." And to this man, whose voice was potential in all the stormy and trying scenes of that early time, some historians give the high honor of making the first formal suggestion of a federal union. It is said that he planted the seed-thought in the mind of Samuel Adams, who became its first great champion. The next day, after holding an interdenominational communion service in his church, he met Samuel Adams, and said to him, with the enthusiasm of a new inspiration: "We have just had a communion of the churches, now let us have a union of states." That is claimed to be the genesis, first of colonial, and afterward of the federal union.

And it is a fact of history that though the genius of a great statesman penned the

JONATHAN MAYHEW

DEMOSTHENES

SAMUEL ADAMS

Declaration of Independence, it was the convincing eloquence of a minister of the gospel that compelled the members of the Continental Congress to affix to it their signature. That minister, a member of the Congress, was the Rev. Dr. Witherspoon, President of Princeton College. The Congress hesitated. The destiny of a nation was suspended upon one hour of agonizing suspense. The historic document lay unrolled upon the table. At that critical moment the venerable President of Princeton arose, and with great emotion uttered these words:

REV. JOHN WITHERSPOON

> To hesitate at this moment is to consent to our own slavery. That notable instrument upon your table, which insures immortality to its author, should be subscribed this very morning by every pen in this house. He that will not respond to its accent and strain every nerve to carry into effect its provisions is unworthy the name of freeman. Whatever I have of property, of reputation, is staked on the issue of this contest; and although these gray hairs must soon descend into the sepulcher, I would infinitely rather that they descend hither by the hand of an executioner than desert at this crisis the sacred cause of my country.

Among the most influential of those early pastors and teachers was the Rev. Alexander Whitaker, who was honored with the title of "the apostle of Virginia." He gave Christian baptism to the Indian princess, Pocahontas, and officiated on the occasion of her marriage. And another distinguished minister in Virginia was a native of Scotland, a man of letters, and one eminently gifted with the leadership, the Rev. James Blair. By his indefatigable labors the college of William and Mary was established, and for forty-nine years he was its able President.

REV. JAMES BLAIR

In New England was Thomas Hooker, whom Cotton Mather called "the incomparable Hooker"—a scholarly graduate of Cambridge and honored with an invitation to sit in the Westminster Assembly, whose ability as a statesman was only equaled by his eloquence as a preacher, his learning as a theologian, and his self-denying toils for his poor sheep in the wilderness. So great was his power that it is said "miracles were attributed to him by his wondering parishioners." But the greatest leader of that early day, a Cambridge scholar and fellow of Emanuel College, was the Rev. John Cotton. Driven from his parish church, St. Botolph's in Lincolnshire, he fled the country, and, "after many narrow escapes," reached Boston in 1633. He soon rose to unrivaled influence, and was called "the Pope of New England." One historian of that time said that whatever John Cotton "delivered in the pulpit was soon put into an order of the court . . . or set up as a practise in the Church." Roger Williams reported the people of New England as saying that "they could hardly believe that God would suffer Mr. Cotton to err." So vast and abiding was his influence as to call

REV. JOHN COTTON

forth from Thomas Carlyle this quaint remark: "John Cotton, his mark, very curiously stamped on the face of this planet, likely to continue for some time." To his genius and abiding influence Longfellow paid this appreciative tribute:

> The lantern of St. Botolph's ceased to burn
> When from the portals of that church he came;
> To be a burning and a shining light,
> Here in the wilderness.

What was said of Oliver Cromwell might have been applied just as truly to John Cotton: that "he was a strong man; in the dark perils of war, in the high places of the field, hope shone in him like a pillar of fire when it had gone out in all others."

But of Thomas Bray, in Maryland, and Jonathan Dickinson, in New Jersey, of whom Erskine said "the British Isles had

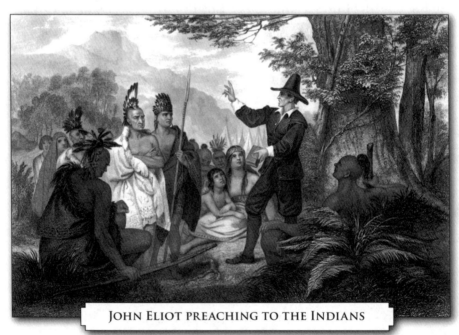

JOHN ELIOT PREACHING TO THE INDIANS

produced no such writer on divinity in the eighteenth century," and John Eliot, the apostle to the Indians, and the two remarkable but quaint brothers, Increase and Cotton Mather, and others who wrought their noble characters into the Christian civilization of that early period, I can not speak at length. A grateful word must be spoken of Jonathan Edwards, the grandest figure in the colonial pulpit. Among the mighty men of the centuries his name will ever have conspicuous mention. As theologian, author, educator, preacher, he impressed this nation and all its generations. "I consider Jonathan Edwards," says Robert Hall, "the greatest of the sons of men. He ranks with the brightest luminaries of the Christian Church, not excluding any country or any age since the apostolic." This marvelous man, who was "a Thomas a Kempis, a Calvin, a Jeremy Taylor in one," has enriched the spiritual and political heritage of the American commonwealth, and "his name invests the middle colonial period with a halo of glory and renown."

Acknowledgement of God in the State Constitutions

I come now to consider the organic laws adopted by the young states soon to form a more perfect union—"an indissoluble union of indestructible states." The constitution of **NEW JERSEY**, framed in 1776, guaranteed to every one the "inestimable privilege of worshiping Almighty God in a manner agreeable to the dictates of his conscience," and then declared that "all persons professing a belief in the faith of any Protestant sect, and who shall demean themselves peaceably under the government, should be capable of being members of either branch of the Legislature, and should fully and freely enjoy every privilege and immunity enjoyed by others, their fellow citizens."

The constitution of **NEW HAMPSHIRE** affirmed "that morality and piety, rightly grounded on evangelical principles, would give the best and greatest security to government," and "that the knowledge of these was most likely to be propagated by the institution of the public worship of the Deity, and public instruction in morality and religion." "The towns," therefore, were authorized and empowered to make proper and adequate provision for the maintenance of "public Protestant teachers of piety, religion, and morality."

The constitution of **DELAWARE** declared that "all persons professing the Christian religion ought forever to enjoy equal rights and privileges," and provided that all persons elected to the Legislature or appointed to any other public office should make the following declaration: "I do profess faith in God the Father, and in Jesus Christ his Son, and the Holy Ghost, one God, blessed forevermore; and I do acknowledge the Holy Scriptures of the Old and New Testaments to be given by divine inspiration."

In the organic law of **NORTH CAROLINA**, adopted about the same time, there was a provision declaring that "no person who should deny the being of God, or the truth of the Protestant religion, or the divine authority of either the Old or New Testament, or who should hold religious principles incompatible with the freedom and safety of the state, should be capable of holding any office or place of trust in the civil government of the state."

The constitution of **GEORGIA**, adopted in 1777, says, "Every officer of the state shall be liable to be called to account by the House of Assembly," and that every member of that House "shall be of the Protestant religion."

SOUTH CAROLINA, in 1778, framed a constitution, which directed the Legislature, at its regular meeting, to "choose by ballot from among themselves, or from the people at large, a governor and commander-in-chief, a lieutenant-governor, and privy council, all of the Protestant religion." It further provided that no man should be eligible to a seat in either branch of the Legislature, "unless he be of the Protestant religion," and positively ordained "that the Christian religion be deemed, and is hereby constituted and declared to be, the established religion of this land."

In 1780 **MASSACHUSETTS** adopted a constitution, in which was the following language:

> That as the happiness of a people, and the good order and preservation of civil government, essentially depend upon piety, religion, and morality; and as these can not be generally diffused through a community but by the institution of the public worship of God and of public instruction in piety, religion, and morality: therefore, to promote their happiness, and

to secure the good order and preservation of their government, the people of this commonwealth have a right to invest their Legislature with power to authorize and require, and the Legislature shall from time to time authorize and require the several towns, parishes, precincts, and other bodies politic, or religious societies, to make suitable provision, at their own expense, for the institution of the public worship of God, and for the support and maintenance of public Protestant teachers of piety, religion, and morality, in all cases where such provision shall not be made voluntarily: and the people of this commonwealth have also a right to, and do, invest their Legislature with authority to enjoin upon all the subjects an attendance upon the instructions of the public teachers aforesaid, at stated times and seasons, if there be any one whose instructions they can conscientiously attend;" and it was also provided that every person "chosen governor, lieutenant-governor, senator, or representative, and accepting the trust," shall solemnly affirm that he "believes the Christian religion, and has a firm persuasion of its truth."

But further investigation is unnecessary to establish the truth of my contention. Such was the structure and dominant spirit of the early colonial institutions. Although reaction soon set in, and many modifications were adopted from time to time to meet the demands of a liberalizing public opinion, those governments "lasted long enough to be the mold in which the civilization of the young states should set and harden."

CHAPTER 4

Christianity and the Nation

I N THE LAST lecture we studied the principles embodied by the colonists in the institutions they established. Attention was directed to the compacts and constitutions they adopted, the laws they enacted, and the social life they created. Having previously analyzed the character of the early settlers of America, and noted the high Christian motive that impelled their coming to these shores, and the divine purpose that dominated their efforts to build here a nation in which they could worship God unmolested, we expected to find their vigorous and aggressive religious principles preeminent in the social and governmental conditions they established. And that expectation was abundantly realized. We discovered that religion chiefly inspired the colonization of this great country, and religion determined the character of government under which those Christian exiles proposed to live. Some of the laws enacted were but transcripts of the divine law, and nothing was allowable that was not sustained by the letter or spirit of the Holy Scriptures. In more than one colony the oath of a public officer was scarcely less than a formal confession of faith. In all

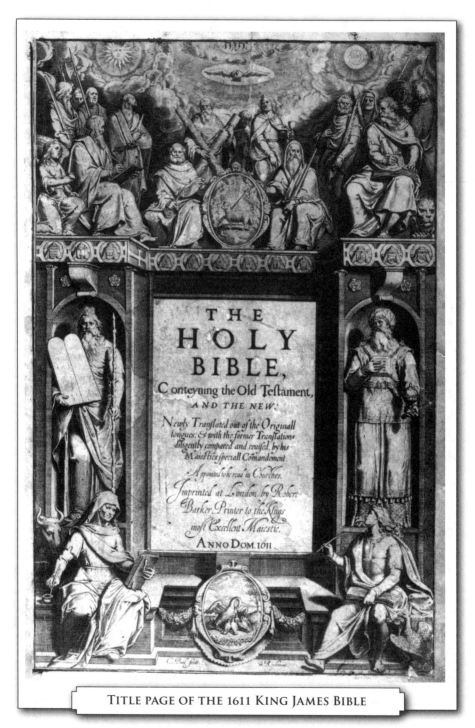

TITLE PAGE OF THE 1611 KING JAMES BIBLE

except two colonies—Rhode Island and Pennsylvania —the Church was established by law, and ministers were supported by public taxation. In several colonies there was a spiritual qualification on the suffrage—only those allowed to vote who were members of the Church. By thus guarding the franchise effort was made to lodge political power only in the hands of good men, and to preserve the government pure from immorality and irreligion. However unwise the measures adopted, we can not but applaud the high purpose of such legislation. They thought it better that the state should be molded by the Church than for the Church to be molded after the state.

In tracing the evolution of those scattered settlements into organized colonies, and then into the dignity and independence of statehood, we noted the informing and guiding influence still exercised by the Christian religion. Though the relaxation of certain regulations was made necessary by the rapid increase of population, and other laws had to be repealed or greatly modified, the distinct Christian and Protestant character of their institutions was carefully preserved. The constitutions of the young states sought to sacredly guard the priceless heritage of the fathers, and some of them reenthroned with emphasis the doctrines of civil and religious liberty that had made the country grow so great and with such majestic speed.

We will now advance from the colonial to the national period of our country's history, and in this chapter study *Christianity and the Nation.* We will ascertain, if possible, how far those granite Christian principles and sturdy faiths of the colonies we have been so eagerly investigating were retained and employed in the nation that was builded. It has been positively affirmed, and by one somewhat eminent in literature, that "the government of the United States is not in any sense founded upon the Christian religion." Is there any historic foundation for that contention, or did the author take counsel of personal desire rather than accepted and authoritative fact? That the latter is true will be triumphantly sustained by the results of a little candid investigation. Did the colonies lose their distinctive religious character when they developed into nationhood? Was there anything in the evolutionary process to strip them of their Christian principles and demand that they be clothed upon with new faiths, or no faith? Was the nation built of new materials, or did the framers of our federal government use the principles and forces already at hand? These and similar inquiries must now be impartially considered and candidly answered.

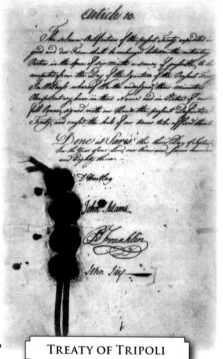

TREATY OF TRIPOLI

That certain adverse influences, notably French infidelity, imported during the war of the Revolution, had a temporary yet strong effect upon our national life must be admitted. To that darkest period of our nation's annals attention will be given. But that those destructive influences were sufficiently potent to change the character of our social life and the type of our governmental institutions, I apprehend, will not be sustained by the facts of history.

Before the national constitution was framed there was a severing of the politico-ecclesiastical ties that had long existed in most of the colonies. But the separation of the Church from the State did not mean the severance of the State from God, or of the nation from Christianity. Some of the colonial states disestablished the Church and passed laws guaranteeing unrestricted freedom of worship before the plan of a constitutional convention had ever taken shape in the mind of any patriot-statesman. Virginia did so two years before the convention met, and fully ten years before all repressive acts against dissenters had been swept from the statute-books. And other colonies took similar action. Those changes came by the logic of events. They were demanded, expected, and could not be resisted.

From such an unauthorized and unscriptural union of Church and State of course evil came. Bancroft states the case clearly in a few well-worded sentences: "Since a particular form of worship had become a part of the civil establishment, irreligion was now to be punished as a civil offence. The state was a model of Christ's kingdom on earth; treason against the civil government was treason against Christ, and, reciprocally, as the gospel had the right paramount, blasphemy, or whatever a jury might call blasphemy, was the highest offense in the catalogue of crimes. To deny any book of the Old or New Testament to be the written and infallible word of God was punished by fine or by stripes, and, in case of obstinacy, by exile or death. Absence from the ministry of the word was punished by fine."

The too close union of Church and State, as population grew and immigration increased, became a source of increasing irritation. It was an unnatural alliance, and has ever

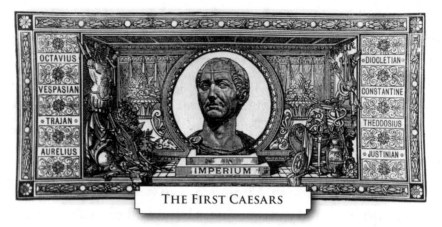

OCTAVIUS

VESPASIAN

TRAJAN

AURELIUS

DIOCLETIAN

CONSTANTINE

THEODOSIUS

JUSTINIAN

IMPERIUM

THE FIRST CAESARS

been an occasion of injury—injury to the Church and peril to the State. Christ and Caesar are at peace, but their kingdoms are independent. They cooperate, but should never unite. The miter and the crown should never encircle the same brow. The crozier and the scepter should never be wielded by the same hand. And whenever the functions of the State have been usurped by the Church, or the offices of the State have been seized and exercised by the Church, Christ and Caesar have alike suffered at the hands of professed but misguided friends.

But the sundering of the ties that bound Church and State too closely together did not drive the nation from Christianity. No such purpose was contemplated and no such action was taken. Their high ambition was not to construct a new nation out of new materials, but to make strong and more enduring the one founded on the faith of their fathers.

> A pure republic, where, beneath the sway
> Of mild and equal laws, framed by themselves,
> One people dwell and own no lord save God.

WASHINGTON PRAYING AT VALLEY FORGE

The scenes connected with the overthrow of British power and the firm establishment of an independent nationhood form some of the most thrilling and brilliant chapters in the annals of America, if not in the world. But not all the heroism was on the high places of the field; and not all the victories were won in the wild shock of battle. There was a heroism of pure faith as well as of high courage. And the one was not less potential than the other. The patriarch kneeling at his family altar, the minister in his pulpit, the devout mother in Israel hiding all these wondrous things of God in her heart, and the words of cheer sent to the front, were not unimportant factors in the final triumph of the colonial arms. Along with the military chieftain's words of command went the ringing appeals and fervent prayers of the ministers of religion. The man of God sat on the mountain-side with hands uplifted in piteous prayer to Heaven, while brave battalions charged with intrepid courage upon their enemies on the plains below. And but for that mountain of prayer there would not have been the glorious victory of the plain.

"The pulpit of the Revolution," a distinguished author says, "was the secret of that moral energy which sustained the republic in its material weakness against superior numbers and discipline and all the powers of England." The intrepid faith of the ministry was as inspiring as the drum-beat of heroic legions led by some gallant commander flushed with the honors of great victory. And all through the history of the American commonwealth the holy men who have ministered at her altars of religion by their exposition and enforcement of the ethics of the Man of Galilee have "connected," says John Quincy Adams, "with one indissoluble bond the principles of civil government with the principles of Christianity."

MINISTER BESTOWS
BLESSING ON MINUTEMAN

And all during that memorable struggle of eight eventful years the Continental Congress, voicing the national faith, often appointed days of fasting and prayer, and repeatedly invited the people to repentance, reformation, and the renewal of their Christian vows. Strange indeed were the passage of such solemn resolutions if they were not an expression of the spiritual hope and faith of the nation. At the very beginning of that long war Congress

ARTICLES OF
CONFEDERATION

formally expressed its desire to "have the people of all ranks and degrees duly impressed with a solemn sense of God's superintending providence, and of their duty to rely in all their lawful enterprises in his aid and direction." In the proclamation of a general fast these words occur: "That they may with united hearts confess and bewail their manifold sins and transgressions, and by a sincere repentance and amendment of life appease His righteous displeasure, and through the merits and mediation of Jesus Christ obtain his pardon and forgiveness." This language reads very much like a pastoral letter issued by some great ecclesiastical synod, conference, or council. Here is a clear, distinct confession of faith in "the merits and mediation of Jesus Christ" by the Congress of the nation, which was the authoritative voice and conscience of the people.

JOHN QUINCY ADAMS

And a few months later another proclamation was issued, which contained this language: "The Congress do also in the most earnest manner, recommend to all the members of the United States, and particularly the officers, civil and military, under them, the exercise of repentance and reformation; and further require of them the strict observance of the articles which forbid profane swearing and all immoralities." Thus with the fervor of apostles did those revolutionary statesmen plead for holiness of conduct, that the nation might be assured of the favor of heaven. They had not read the history of Israel in vain, and knew that it is righteousnes that exalteth a nation.

In 1777 Congress called the colonies to earnest prayer, and begged "that with one heart and voice the good people may express the grateful feelings of their hearts, and consecrate themselves to the service of their Divine Benefactor; and that, together with their sincere acknowledgments and offerings, they may join the penitent confession of their manifold sins, whereby they have forfeited every favor, and their earnest supplication that it may please God, through the merits of Jesus Christ, mercifully to forgive and blot them out of remembrance; that it may please him graciously to afford his blessings on the governments of these states respectively, and prosper the public council of the whole; to inspire our commanders, both by land and sea, and all under them, with that wisdom and fortitude which may render them fit instruments, under the government of Almighty God, to secure to these United States the greatest of all blessings—independence and peace . . . to take schools and seminaries for education, so necessary for cultivating the principles of true liberty, virtue, and piety, under his nurturing hand, and to prosper the means of religion for the promotion and enlargement of that kingdom which consisteth in righteousness, peace, and joy in the Holy Ghost."

THE FIRST CONTINENTAL CONGRESS

In 1799, by resolution of Congress, the people are called upon to pray: "That God would grant to his Church the plentiful effusions of divine grace, and pour out his Holy Spirit on all ministers of the gospel; that he would bless and prosper the means of education and spread the light of Christian knowledge throughout the remotest corners of the earth." And similar appeals were made in 1780, 1781, and 1782. Certainly there was no lack of religious faith in that body of Christian patriots.

Before considering the convention of 1787 and the constitution then drafted and afterward ratified by the several states —that instrument which has been characterized as the most remarkable uninspired document ever struck from the human brain by a single blow—I invite you to take account of some adverse currents that came in like a flood upon our country.

The independence of the colonies was achieved at a dreadful cost: the threatened loss of our national faith. With the triumph of arms there came the fall of public morals. The French allies proved to be dangerous friends. They fought for our success in the field, but they poisoned our national faith. They injected the virus of an aggressive and unblushing infidelity into our country that came near working its ruin. Its blight was seen and felt everywhere. The churches suffered, homes were destroyed, colleges were poisoned, the Sabbath was desecrated, and public morals were polluted. The churches reported "the lamentable decay of vital piety, the degeneracy of manners, the want of public spirit, and the general prevalence of vice and immorality." Some public men became blatant and blasphemous in their infidelity. Gen. Dearborn, afterward Secretary of War in Jefferson's cabinet, is reported to have pointed on one occasion at a Christian church and said: "So long as those temples stand we can not hope for order and good government." Passing a church-building in Connecticut

EDMUND RANDOLPH

on another occasion, he remarked with scornful tone and sneering lip: "Look at that painted nuisance." Edmund Randolph became a deist, but afterward returned to his evangelical faith. Thomas Jefferson became very liberal in his creed, probably a unitarian, but never lost a firm faith in God and his providence. And many others felt the contagion. But the great body of patriots and statesmen stood firmly by the faith of their fathers. Patrick Henry said he abhorred infidelity, and wrote a book, though never published, in reply to Paine's *Age of Reason*. And so Washington and others boldly resisted the deadly plague.

Devereux Jarrett, of Virginia, drew a vivid sketch of the moral degeneracy of the times, and charged it to "the prevalence of the spirit of the French Revolution." The General Assembly of the Presbyterian Church in 1798 sent out a pastoral letter, full of alarm and entreaty: "We perceive with pain and fearful apprehension a general dereliction of religious principle and practise among our fellow-citizens, a visible and prevailing impiety and contempt for the laws and institutions of religion, and an abounding infidelity which, in many instances, tends to atheism itself. The profligacy and corruption of the public morals have advanced with a progress proportioned to our declension in religion."

Infidel clubs were organized, and publications like Paine's *Age of Reason*

DR. TIMOTHY DWIGHT

were scattered broadcast over the land. The colleges of the country became the hotbeds of a shallow but noisy skepticism. But a reaction, after a time, set in, led by Dr. Dwight, President of Yale College, and others of great influence in Church and State, and this great nation, born of religious convictions and built by Christian faith and principle, swung safely back to the integrity of her divine inheritance.

When, in 1800, President John Adams received a letter from Germany, proposing to send over to this country "a company of schoolmasters, painters, poets, etc., all of them disciples

JOHN ADAMS

of Thomas Paine," he made prompt and emphatic reply as follows: "I had rather countenance the introduction of Ariel and Caliban with a troupe of spirits the most mischievous from the fairy-land." And in a proclamation shortly thereafter, setting forth the dangers threatening the young republic, he thus reannounced the national faith: "The most precious interests of the United States are still held in jeopardy by the hostile designs and insidious arts of a foreign nation (France), as well as by the dissemination among them of those principles subversive of the foundation of all religious, moral, and social obligations, that have produced incalculable mischiefs and misery in other countries."

The one man whose coming to America was more to be deplored than any other was Thomas Paine. His political writings gave him fame and influence, but his coarse and vulgar skepticism made him in the end the shunned and despised of all American decency. Though regretting the occasion for any reference to such moral and political vileness, as a study in personal irreligion and an object-lesson to the young who may be tempted to toy with the faiths of the soul, I here introduce a graphic description of his last days by an excellent historian. That horrible old age and despised memory are the bitter harvest of his own skeptical sowing.

McMaster, in his *History of the People of the United States*, thus describes Tom Paine:

> We doubt whether any name in our Revolutionary history, not excepting that of Benedict Arnold, is quite so odious as the name of Thomas Paine. Arnold was a traitor; Paine was an infidel. . . . Since the day when the *Age of Reason* came forth from the press the number of infidels has increased much more rapidly than before that book was written. The truth is, he was one of the most remarkable men of his time. It would be a difficult matter to find anywhere another such compound of baseness and nobleness, of goodness and badness, of greatness and littleness, of so powerful a mind left unbalanced and led astray by the worst of animal passions….Of all humankind he is the filthiest and nastiest, and his disgusting habits grew upon him with his years. In his old age, when the frugal gifts of two states which remembered his good work had placed him beyond immediate want, he became a sight to behold. It was rare that he was sober; it was still rarer that he washed himself, and he suffered his nails to grow till, in the

THOMAS PAINE

language of one who knew him well, they resembled the claws of birds. What gratitude was he did not know.

I come now to study the federal charter—the "supreme law of the land"—adopted by the historic convention of 1787 in the city of Philadelphia, and its relation to the Christian religion. Was any action taken by that grave body of great statesmen that was intended directly or indirectly to repudiate the pronounced Christian faith of the colonial fathers? Their courage had been tested in the storm of war, and now their ambitions could only be inspired by the loftiest patriotism—the completion of a work so gloriously begun. James Madison, who preserved the debates of that memorable convention, and who

JAMES MADISON

was conspicuous in its deliberations, said that "there never was an assembly of men, charged with a great and arduous trust who were purer in their motives, or more exclusively or anxiously devoted to the object committed to them, than were the members of the federal convention of 1787 to the object of devising and proposing a constitutional system which should best supply the defects of that which it was to replace, and best secure the permanent liberty and happiness of their country."

George Washington sat in the President's chair, and all the deliberations of that serious body were as solemn as the synod of a great Church in a time of spiritual crisis. The burdens of a nation and the centuries were upon their already chafed and weary shoulders. Great were the difficulties they had to meet, and most momentous were the problems they had to

CONSTITUTIONAL CONVENTION

solve. One graphic and pathetic scene in that convention is painfully suggestive of the tremendous burden of anxiety that sometimes threatened the defeat of all their patriotic counsels and the loss of all the splendid fruits of victory on the field of battle. I refer to the appearance of Dr. Franklin—a veteran of eighty-three years of age—and his memorable appeal for prayer. The speech of Benjamin Franklin in the constitutional convention, supporting a motion for daily prayers to God in the body, is a notable historic fact, when we consider the great man who uttered it and the greater occasion which suggested it. It was an hour of gloom. Divided opinion, sectional animosities, and some personal estrangements threatened to defeat the patriotic purpose of their solemn assembling. But little progress had been made, and many began to fear that differences were irreconcilable and agreement was impossible. In that hour Dr. Benjamin Franklin, not supposed to be evangelical in his opinions, arose, but, too feeble to stand long on his feet, asked his colleague to read the manuscript speech he had prepared. From that address I take these suggestive sentences:

In the beginning of the contest with Great Britain, when we were sensible of danger, we had daily prayer in this room for the divine protection. Our prayers, sir, were heard, and they were graciously answered. All of us who were engaged in the struggle must have observed frequent instances of a superintending Providence in our favor. To that kind Providence

BENJAMIN FRANKLIN

we owe this happy opportunity of consulting in peace on the means of establishing our future national felicity. And have we now forgotten that powerful Friend? Or do we imagine that we no longer need his assistance?

"I have lived, sir, a long time, and the longer I live the more convincing proofs I see of this truth: that God governs in the affairs of men. And if a sparrow can not fall to the ground without his notice, is it possible that an empire can rise without his aid? We have been assured, sir, in the sacred writings that, 'except the Lord build the house, they labor in vain that build it.' I firmly believe this, and I also believe that without his concurring aid we shall succeed, in this political building, no better than the builders of Babel.

Though the motion was not adopted, and the secret sessions were not opened and closed with invocation and benediction,

THE UNITED STATES CONSTITUTION

influential members were careful to assign other reasons than indifference to religion or lack of faith in the superintending providence of God.

Now inasmuch as in the constitution of the United States the name of God is not mentioned, and the references to religion are rather negative than positive, it has been charged that the American commonwealth has an atheistical organic law. That question we will now investigate, for the Christian character of our nation is involved therein. And in the study of the same one fact should be borne in mind: "*The constitution did not create a nation or its religion and institutions.*" It was framed for the better protection of those already existing, and under a government of the people, by the people, and for the people.

The constitution of the United States provides that *"No religious test shall ever be required as a qualification to any office or public trust under the United States."*

The first amendment to that constitution reads as follows: "Congress shall make no law respecting an establishment of religion, or prohibiting the free exercise thereof; *or abridging the freedom of speech, or of the press; or the right of the people peaceably to assemble, and to petition the government for a redress of grievance."*

This Article VI., paragraph 3, abolishes all religious tests in the conduct of civil affairs, and secures the freedom and independence of the State from ecclesiastical domination and interference. But the first amendment, adopted in response to the demand of many of the states as a condition of their ratifying the constitution itself, is a more positive declaration, and constitutes what is known as a bill of rights. This is the full and absolute guarantee of perfect religious liberty. Many of the principles embodied in the constitution have been handed down from the

DR. PHILIP SCHAFF

days of Magna Charta, but, as Dr. Philip Schaff has observed, "it was left for America to abolish forever the tyranny of a State religion, and to secure the most sacred of all rights and liberties to all her citizens - the liberty of religion and the free exercise thereof." Thus the right of individuality and the sovereignty of the conscience were vindicated and protected from outside interference, and the power was forever withheld from the federal government to invade the inner sanctuary of the human soul.

The purpose of that article was not to renounce Christianity or give countenance to infidelity or any pagan religion, but to exclude all rivalry among Christian denominations and "prevent any national ecclesiastical establishment which should give to a hierarchy the exclusive patronage of the national government." It was not antichristian, but antisectarian. It would not favor one branch of the Church of Christ over another. The Episcopalians were the predominant sect in some states, the Presbyterians in others, the Congregationalists in others, the Quakers in at least one, while several were nearly evenly balanced numerically in others. It was eminent statesmanship, therefore, to eliminate ecclesiastical ambitions and sectarian jealousies from the civil government, by giving the same reverent recognition and sacred protection to all alike. All Churches were put on an equal footing before the supreme law of the nation. "Liberty of all is the best guarantee of the liberty of each."

I know of no more critical and luminous statement of the true religious purpose of the framers of the constitution than these words by an able writer on constitutional law: "Consistent with themselves, the people of 1787 meant by the Federal arrangement nothing but a new and larger organization of government *on principles already familiar* to the country. The state governments were not broad enough for national purposes, and the old confederation was deficient in central power. It was only to remedy these two defects, not of principle but of distributive adjustment, that the public mind addressed itself; innovation, to any other end, was never thought of, least of all in reference to religion, a thing utterly apart from the whole design. So that, admitting that the constitution framed on that occasion does not in terms proclaim itself a Christian document, what then? Does it proclaim itself unchristian? For if it is merely silent in the matter, law and reason both tell us that its religious character is to be looked for by interpretation among the people who fashioned it, a people Christian by profession and by genealogy; what is more, by deed of fundamental legislation that can not deceive."

And from the highest authorities, that might be multiplied almost indefinitely, we are left in no doubt that this was the view taken by all the constitutional fathers, and which found clear expression in our organic law. The supreme care was not to restrain, but to encourage and increase the rapid spread and lasting sway of our Christian religion throughout the American commonwealth.

The only limitation ever placed upon the largest assertion of religious liberty by the national government was the passage of a law against plural marriage which is a tribue to Christian religion. This law, so necessary to the sanctity of the home and the purity of society, has its origin and divine imperative only in the New Testament. So the enactment of that prohibition is an inspiration of the ethics of Christianity. And no appeal to any religious tenet or belief is allowed to contravene that express statute which came first from the Man of Galilee.

The validity and constitutionality of that law has been tested before the Supreme Court of the United States, and sustained at every point. The case came up from the territory of Utah, the accused pleading the doctrines of the Mormon Church and the constitutional guarantee of religious liberty as his defense. As the opinion rendered is the first judicial definition of the bounds of the religious liberty guaranteed by the constitution, I shall quote a few passages therefrom. The opinion of the court was delivered by Chief Justice Waite, and is as follows:

Laws are made for the government of actions; and while they can not interfere with mere religious beliefs and opinions, they may with practises. Suppose one believed that human sacrifices were a necessary part of religious worship. Would it be seriously contended that the civil government under which he lived could not interfere to prevent a sacrifice? Or if a wife religiously believed it was her duty to burn herself upon the funeral pile of her dead husband, would it be beyond the power of the civil government to prevent her carrying her belief into practise?

CHIEF JUSTICE
MORRISON WAITE

So here, as a law of the organization of society under the exclusive dominion of the United States, it is provided that plural marriages shall not be allowed. Can a man exercise his practises to the contrary, because of his religious belief? To permit this would be to make the professed doctrines of religious belief superior to the law of the land, and in effect to permit every citizen to become a law unto himself. Government could exist only in name under such circumstances.

It is an interesting historic fact also that the National Congress has officially favored and approved the Holy Scriptures, and the authorized Protestant version and revision of the same.

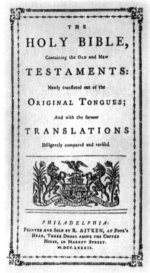

The Continental Congress in 1782 and the United States 1882, just one century apart, passed specific resolutions in regard to the Holy Scriptures. Bibles becoming very scarce during the war of the Revolution, Congress was petitioned to publish the book. The petition was not granted, on account of the difficulty in procuring types and paper, but authority was given to import twenty thousand copies from Europe. And that same Congress appointed a committee to examine the first English Bible published in America. The committee submitted it to examination by the two chaplains, Rev. W. White and Rev. George Duffield, and, on their recommendation, Congress approved "the pious and laudable undertaking" and recommended it "to the inhabitants of the United States."

In 1882 Congress passed an act exempting from customary duties over two thousand copies of the Revised Version of the Holy Scriptures, printed on the university presses of Oxford and Cambridge.

And in an ordinance adopted by

REV. GEORGE DUFFIELD

Congress July 13, 1787, for the government of the Northwest territory, a section then under entire control of the federal authority, it is declared that "Religion, morality, and knowledge are necessary to good government and the happiness of mankind."

This, then, is a Christian nation, constructed by a Christian people, and for Christian ends, their religion the common law of the land. The Christian religion is so inwrought into the laws of the United States that they can only be wisely interpreted by the light of revelation. A distinguished American jurist has said that "the best features of the common law, if not derived from, have at least been improved and strengthened by, the prevailing religion and the teachings of the sacred Book, especially those that regard the family and social relations." And Chief Justice Cooley, in his great work on "Constitutional Limitations," has given this opinion, which has all the weight of the highest judicial authority: "The Christian religion was always recognized in the administration of the common law;

DANIEL WEBSTER

and so far as that law continues to be the law of the land, the fundamental principles of that religion must continue to be recognized in the same sense and to the same extent."

Daniel Webster, the great "expounder of the constitution," in the celebrated Girard will case before the Supreme Court of the United States, in February, 1844, most ably advocated the doctrine that Christianity is the common law of this nation. He sought to set aside the munificent devise of Stephen Girard for the establishment of a college in Philadelphia, on the ground that the testator had discriminated against the Christian religion, even going so far as to provide that no minister of the gospel should ever be admitted within the walls of the institution. With imperial eloquence he discussed the vital connection between religion and education, and triumphantly showed that he who would profanely divorce the two made a ruthless assault upon the common law of the land. Though somewhat lengthy, I must quote the following splendid passage:

> It is the same in Pennsylvania as elsewhere: the general principles and public policy are sometimes established by constitutional provisions, sometimes by legislative enactments, sometimes by judicial decisions, sometimes by general consent. But however they may be established, there is nothing that we look for with more certainty than the general principle that Christianity is a part of the law of the land. This was the case among the Puritans of New England, the Episcopalians of the Southern States, the Pennsylvania Quakers, the Baptists, the mass of the followers of Whitefield and Wesley, and the Presbyterians; all brought and all adopted this great truth, and all have sustained it. And where there is any religious sentiment amongst men at all, this sentiment incorporates itself with the law. *Everything declares it.* The massive cathedral of the Catholic; the Episcopalian church, with its lofty spire pointing heavenward; the plain temple of the Quaker; the log church of the hardy pioneer of the wilderness; the mementoes and memorials around and about us; the consecrated graveyards, their tombstones and epitaphs, their silent vaults, their moldering contents—all attest it. *The dead*

prove it as well as the living. The generations that are gone before speak it, and pronounce it from the tomb. We feel it. All, all proclaim that Christianity, general, tolerant Christianity, Christianity independent of sects and parties, that Christianity to which the sword and fagot are uknown, general, tolerant Christianity, is the law of the land."

In a celebrated case in the state of New York, in which a man was charged with blasphemy, the Supreme Bench held the validity and constitutionality of the law. Chief Justice Kent, the distinguished author of the "Commentaries on American Law," delivered the opinion of the court. He said:

> ... *We are a Christian people*, and the morality of the country is deeply ingrafted upon Christianity. . . . This declaration (of the New York constitution in favor of religious liberty) never meant to withdraw religion in general, and with it the best sanctions of moral and social obligation, from all consideration and motion of law. To construe it as breaking down the common law barriers against licentious, wanton, and impious attacks upon Christianity itself would be an enormous perversion of its meaning.

Judge Theodore W. Dwight, a distinguished jurist, and for many years the learned dean of the Columbia Law School, New York, gave this able opinion on the subject: "It is well settled by decisions in the courts of the leading states of the Union—*e.g.*, New York, Pennsylvania, and Massachusetts—that Christianity is a part of the common law of the state. Its recognition is shown in the administration of oaths in the courts of justice, in the rules which punish those who wilfully blaspheme, in the observance of Sunday, in the prohibition of profanity, in the legal establishment of permanent charitable trusts, and in the legal principles which control a parent in the education and training of his children. One of the American courts (that of Pennsylvania) states the law in this manner: 'Christianity is and always

THEODORE W. DWIGHT

has been a part of the common law of this state—Christianity without the spiritual artillery of European countries—not Christianity founded on any particular religious tenets, not Christianity with an established church and tithes and spiritual courts, but Christianity with liberty of conscience to all men.' The American states adopted these principles from the common law of England, rejecting such portions of the English law on this subject as were not suited to their customs and institutions. *Our national development has in it the best and purest elements of historic Christianity, as related to the government of states.* Should we tear Christianity out of our law, we would rob our law of its fairest jewels, we would deprive it of its richest treasures, we would arrest its growth, and bereave it of its capacity to adapt itself to the progress in culture, refinement, and morality of those for whose benefit it properly exists."

The influence of Christianity is of final authority in the proceedings and decisions of our courts of justice. The testimony of witnesses is rejected if the solemnity of an oath is not sustained by belief in the God of heaven. The judge is compelled to inquire: "Do you believe in a God? Do you believe in a future state of rewards and punishments?" If the witness answers in the negative, his testimony is incompetent in the determination of any judicial question, however trivial or important. Thus the administration of law depends upon our holy religion—confidence in human veracity—a confidence necessary to the business of the state and the judicial determination of questions in controversy—grounds upon religious character. The state has to resort to the individual conscience. A judicial oath supposes a conscience sensitive to the issues of an eternal judgment, to give it solemnity and moral weight.

And this doctrine has been fundamental in the jurisprudence and governmental administration of all nations. It is a fact that when infidelity had destroyed the national faith of Greece, and "there was no god to swear by," her officials became corrupt, and the proud republic tottered to its ruin. Rome prospered as the religious convictions of

GEORGE WASHINGTON'S THANKSGIVING PROCLAMATION, 1789

FIRST PARAGRAPH OF WASHINGTON'S PROCLAMATION:

"Whereas it is the duty of all Nations to acknowledge the providence of Almighty God, to obey his will, to be grateful for his benefits, and humbly to implore his protection and favor, and whereas both Houses of Congress have by their joint Committee requested me 'to recommend to the People of the United States a day of public thanksgiving and prayer to be observed by acknowledging with grateful hearts the many signal favors of Almighty God especially by affording tham an opportunity peaceably to establish a form of government for their safety and happiness.'"

the people were most acute and the authority of conscience was most respected. If a Roman soldier violated his oath, even death in battle did not arrest judgment against him. His crime was thought to pursue him into the spirit world and there "confront him at the tribunal of his infernal judges, Minos, Rhadamanthus, and AEacus, whose sentence it would receive to eternal perdition." No wonder, under the discipline of such faith in the rewards of the future, Rome attained to imperial grandeur.

And the official acts of the Presidents of the United States, in their proclamations appointing days of thanksgiving or fasting, and in their addresses to the people, have paid reverent tribute to our national faith.

The inaugural address of George Washington, as the first President of this young republic, breathes the humblest and holiest spirit of dependence upon God, and expresses the nation's faith in his all-wise guidance and care. He recognizes the hand of God in the formation of the government, and prays for his continued direction and perpetual benediction. He says:

It would be peculiarly improper to omit, in this first official act, my fervent supplication to that almighty Being who rules over the universe, who presides in the councils of nations, and whose providential aid can supply every human defect, that his benediction may consecrate to the liberties and happiness of the people of the United States a government instituted by themselves for these essential purposes, and may enable every instrument employed in its administration to execute with success the functions allotted to his charge. In tendering this homage to the great Author of every public and private good, I assure myself that it expresses your sentiments not less than my own, nor those of my fellow citizens at large less than neither. No people can be bound to acknowledge and adore the invisible Hand which conducts the affairs of men more than the people of the United States. Every step by which they have advanced to the character of an independent nation seems to have been distinguished by some token of providential agency.

INAUGURATION OF
GEORGE WASHINGTON

And in the closing sentences of this able and patriotic address the "father of his country" thus refers again to the subject which seemed to be the burden of his great soul - the nation's dependence upon Almighty God for past achievements and all future glory: "Having thus imparted to you my sentiments as they have been awakened by the occasion which brings us together, I shall take my present leave; but not without resorting once more to the benign Parent of the human race, in humble supplication that, since he has pleased to favor the American people with opportunities for deliberating in perfect tranquillity, and dispositions for deciding with unparalleled unanimity on a form of government for the security of their union, and the advancement of their happiness; so his divine blessing may be equally conspicuous in the enlarged views, the temperate consultations, and the wise measures on which the success of this government must depend."

And in his matchless farewell address, a masterful state paper that will be read with increasing reverence and appreciation to the last generation of American patriots, an address which had all the sanctity and solemnity of a last will and testament, he speaks again with the favor of an apostle of his country's indebtedness to our holy religion. He says:

Of all the dispositions and habits which lead to political prosperity, religion and morality are indispensable supports. In vain would that man claim the tribute of patriotism who should labor to subvert these great pillars of human happiness, these firmest props of the duties of men and citizens. The mere politician, equally with the pious man, ought to respect and cherish them. A volume could not trace all their connections with private and public felicity. Let it simply be asked: Where is the security for property, for reputation, for life, if the sense of religious obligation desert the oaths which are the instruments of investigation in courts of justice? And let us with caution indulge the supposition that morality can be maintained without religion. Whatever may be conceded to the influence of refined education on minds of peculiar structure, reason and experience both forbid us to expect that national morality can prevail in exclusion of religious principle.

Days of thanksgiving have been officially and regularly appointed, by all the Presidents from Washington to McKinley, except Jefferson and Jackson, who, not from a sense of indifference but because of expressed doubt as to whether they had authority, under, the constitution, declined to make such appointments. So by this and other official deliverances, and by the legislative history of the national and state governments, we are impressed with the utterance of Goldwin Smith: "Not democracy in America, but free Christianity in America, is the real key to the study of the people and their institutions."

ANDREW JACKSON

And that the faith of our fathers yet abides among the sons of the mighty is happily illustrated in this suggestive incident: When a committee of the Lake Mohawk Conference visited President Cleveland, a few years ago, in the interest of the Indians, the President, among other things, gave expression to this wise sentiment:

No matter what I may do; no matter what you may do; no matter what Congress may do; no matter what may be done for the education of the Indian, after all, the solution of the Indian question rests in the gospel of Christ.

And to this volume of convincing testimony, the testimony of American statesmen, scholars, historians, and divines, I beg to give the calm judgment of two great political writers on the other side of the Atlantic.

Alexis de Tocqueville, in his *Democracy in America*, one of the ablest and most philosophic discussions of our political institutions by any foreigner, thus refers to Christianity as the formative and mightiest influence in our national life:

There is no country in the whole world in which the Christian religion retains a greater influence over the souls of men than in America, and there can be no greater proof of its utility, and of its conformity to human nature, than that its influence is most powerfully felt over the most enlightened and freest nation of the earth. . . . Religion in America takes no direct part in the government of society, but it must, nevertheless, be regarded as *the foremost of the political institutions*

of that country, for if it does not impart a taste for freedom, it facilitates the use of free institutions. I am certain that the Americans *hold religion to be indispensable to the maintenance of republican institutions.* This opinion is not peculiar to a class of citizens or to a party, but it belongs to the whole nation and to every rank of society.

And a more recent foreign student of our national institutions, the distinguished statesman, Prof. James Bryce, of England, in his "American Commonwealth," reaffirms with emphasis the generous judgment of the eloquent Frenchman. He says:

> It was religious zeal and religious conscience which led to the founding of the New England colonies two centuries and a half ago—those colonies whose spirit has in such large measure passed into the whole nation. Religion and conscience have been a constantly active force in the American commonwealth ever since.

JAMES BRYCE

I return, therefore, to the proposition announced at the beginning of this lecture—the separation of Church and State was not the separation of the nation from religion. Christianity is now, and ever has been, the firmest pillar of our civil and political institutions. The State needs far more the protection of the Church than the Church needs the protection of the State. On the faith of our fathers, I do believe, rests the hope of this republic.

CHAPTER 5

Christian Education in the American Commonwealth

I SHALL NOW SPEAK on a subject not strictly necessary to the logical connection of the line of argument we have pursued, but strikingly illustrative of the principles advocated and the conclusions reached. Our studies have disclosed the fact that this is a Christian nation—that Christianity is wrought into the very bone and fiber and blood of our civil and social institutions, and, indeed, has become the common law of the land. In this chapter we will proceed with our investigation of Christian influences upon our national institutions, and study Christian Education in the American Commonwealth.

This will not be a plea for Christian education or a discussion of the great principles involved therein, which should always have the preeminence in Church and State. I shall not consider the claims of education upon American Christians and patriots, and its

BRONZE PLAQUE, U.S. CAPITOL

vital relation to the progress and prominency of our grand republic. It is true that the economic, industrial political, and moral well-being of the nation are largely dependent upon the character and extent of the education provided for the people. But into that broad and inviting field we will not enter to-day. The purpose of this lecture is to briefly sketch the history of Christian education in the American commonwealth, and let the eloquent facts be their own convincing argument. It is well for us to be reminded whence came our great educational systems and enterprises, and by whom they have been so carefully nurtured and guided. We should know to whom the America of to-day is so great a debtor. If it shall appear that the much-lauded educational spirit of our country was generated and nourished by the Christian Church, and that the right training of American youth has been almost entirely promoted by the Church and ministry, that fact ought to serve as an efficient corrective of certain fatal tendencies among some modern educators and their friends. We ought to be very hesitant in consenting to an elimination of the influences that have created and organized the vast educational system of this nation.

The spirit of Protestantism is the spirit of enlightenment, and has ever been the promoter and pioneer of education. It is a fact of history, that with every revival of religion there has been a revival of letters. A quickened spiritual life in the Church has inspired the nation with an increased mental activity. Dr. Dorchester has suggestively observed that:

> The great Reformation allied itself with the universities. Wyclif, Tyndale, Luther, Melanchthon, Farel, and Calvin turned their lecture-rooms into

REFORMERS TRANSLATING THE BIBLE, 1532

preaching-places, and Wittenburg, Heidelburg, the great Sorbonne, Oxford, Cambridge, and Edinburgh, with their thousands of students, made those countries Protestant.

We had reason to expect, therefore, that the sturdy reformers who became the first colonists of America would be the ardent friends of the best education. A large proportion of the ministers who accompanied the brave pioneers were men of the highest culture, and some had become distinguished in scholarship and literature.

WORCESTER COLLEGE OF OXFORD

Within ten years after the coming of Winthrop and his noble company not less than twenty thousand Englishmen made their homes in this new world. Among them were about eighty ministers, fully one-half of whom were graduates of Oxford and Cambridge. These men, of course, became the leaders in all educational movements, and to them and their colaborers and successors this great republic is indebted for the ardent spirit and the elaborate schemes of our national enlightenment. They very early championed a system of schools, as they said, "to the end that learning may not be buried in the graves of our forefathers in Church and commonwealth."

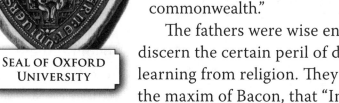

SEAL OF OXFORD
UNIVERSITY

The fathers were wise enough to discern the certain peril of divorcing learning from religion. They accepted the maxim of Bacon, that "In knowledge without love there is ever something of malignity," and provided that the schools they established should be the homes of serious and sanctified learning. They insisted that intellectual culture and spiritual principle must be bound in immortal wedlock. God hath joined them together, and it is fatal profanity to put them asunder.

Those were very straightforward and luminous words of Prof. Huxley on this momentous subject. A better statement I have not seen:

I hold that any system of education which attempts to deal only with the intellectual side of a child's nature, and leaves the rest untouched, will prove a delusion and a snare, just as likely to produce a crop of unusually astute scoundrels as anything else. In my belief, unless a child be taught not only morality but religion, education will come to very little. I believe, further, that, in the present chaotic state of men's thoughts on these subjects, the only practical method of not altogether excluding religion from the education of the masses is to let them read the Bible, and permit the many noble thoughts and deeds mirrored there to sink into their hearts.

The purpose of this chapter is to show that education in the American commonwealth, whether in primary, secondary, or collegiate schools, "owes," as a historian has properly acknowledged, "almost everything to religion."

The Motivation Behind Education in Colonial America

The common school system of the United States, now so highly prized and so distinguishing a feature of the educational scheme of the nation, owes its origin to the Church. The Christian colonists first devised and fostered it, and made distinctive religious teaching therein the chiefest concern. At Dorchester, where the plan was adopted in 1645, elaborate rules were given for the government of the school. A few must be here given:

> 4. Every second day in the weeke he shall call his schollers togeither betweene 12 and one of the Clock to examine them what they have learned on the Saboath day preceding at wch tyme also he shall take notice of any misdemeanor or outrage that any of his schollers shall have committed on the Saboath, to the end that at somme convenient tyme due Admonition and

Correction may be administered by him according as the nature and qualitie of the offence shall require, at wch sayd examination any of the Elders or other Inhabitants that please may bee present, to behold his religious care herein, and to give there Countenance and approbation of the same.

7. Every six day of the weeke at 2 of the Clock in the afternoone, he shall catechise his schollers in the principles of the Christian religion, either in some catechisme wch the Wardens shall provide and present, or in defect thereof in some other.

THE WESTMINSTER CATECHISM, 1832

8. And because all man's indeavor wthout the blessing of God must needs bee fruitlesse and unsuccessful, theirfore, It is to be a chief prte of the schoolmrs religious cars to commend his schollers and his Labours amongst them unto God by prayer morning and evening, taking care that his schollers doe revrendly attend during the same.

This is said to be the first public provision in the world for a free school supported by a direct taxation on the inhabitants of the town. The teacher was required to equally and impartially review and instruct the children who had a right to attend, "whither there parents bee pore or rich;" and it was left to the "discretion of the Elders and 'seven men' for the time being whether maydes shall be taught with the boyes or not."

Education at The New Haven Colony

The New Haven colony, through the "general court," as early as 1641, voted "that a free schoole be set up this towne, and our pastor, Mr. Davenport, together with the magistrates, shall consider whatt yearly allowance is meet to be given to itt out of the common stock of the towne, and allso whatt rules and orders are meet to be observed in and about the same." In a recent history of education in Connecticut there is this reference to that religious beginning of public schools in the colony:

> We note here, in this early record of a Connecticut school, the supervision by the clergyman which has continued until the present, causing even now the clergymen in a village to be chosen school visitors.

Other towns followed this good example. In 1646 Guilford had a school, with Rev. John Higginson as teacher, and shortly

WILLIAM PENN'S WELCOME AT HIS FIRST VISIT TO HIS COLONY

thereafter Milford "made provision in a comfortable way."

A plan for public education was adopted in the very beginning of the Pennsylvania colony. It found conspicuous mention in the first draft of proprietary government drawn up by William Penn in 1682. The founding of Philadelphia the next year was signalized by the establishment of a school. To an amended charter granted by Penn in 1711 there is this preamble: "*Whereas,* the prosperity and welfare of any people depend, in a great measure, upon the good education of youth and their early introduction in the *principles of true religion and virtue,* and qualifying them to serve their country and themselves by breeding them in reading, writing, and learning of languages and useful arts and sciences, suitable to their sex, age, and degree, which can not be effected, in any manner, so well as by erecting public schools for the purpose aforesaid."

And so, if time allowed, I could show that a similar religious spirit, like another angel of the annunciation, proclaimed the being and mission of the schools in all the colonies. The story of one is the history of all. To the Church, the school owed its birth; and to the minister, the children of almost every parish had to look for intellectual training as well as spiritual instruction.

The academic schools of the colonies sprang from the same powerful religious conviction. In 1647, less than twenty-seven years after its settlement, the General Court of the Massachusetts Bay colony passed the following order, the preamble of which indicates the high Christian purpose of these devout sons of a pure Protestantism:

It being one chief object of the old deluder, Satan, to keep men from the knowledge of the Scriptures, as in former times by keeping them in an unknown tongue, so in these latter times by persuading from the use of tongues, that so at least the true sense and meaning of the original might be clouded by false glosses of saint-seeming devices; that learning may not be buried in the grave of our fathers in the Church and commonwealth, the Lord assisting our endeavors.

It is therefore *ordered* that every township in this jurisdiction, after the Lord has increased them to the number of fifty householders, shall then forthwith appoint one within their town to teach all such children as shall resort to him to write and read; whose wages shall be paid, either by the parents or masters of such children or by the inhabitants in general, by way of supply, as the major part of those that order the prudentials of the town shall appoint; provided, those that send their children be not oppressed by paying much more than they can have them taught for in other towns; and it is further ordered, that when any town shall increase to the number of one hundred families or householders, they shall set up a grammar-school, the master thereof being able to instruct youth so far as they may be fitted for the university; provided, that if any town neglect the performance hereof above one year, that every such town shall pay five pounds to the next school till they shall perform this order.

Such was the original spiritual purpose of grammar-schools, now so important a feature of the elaborate educational system of the United States. And for two centuries or more most all of such secondary institutions of the country were under the direction and instruction of ministers of the gospel representing the different evangelical denominations.

Educational Methods in The Virginia Colony

The Virginia colony, as early as 1619, recommended "that each town, borough, and hundred should procure by just means a certain number of children (natives), to be brought up; that the most towardly of these should be fitted for college." Thus it will be seen that almost at the beginning of the Jamestown settlement efforts were made to provide ample

educational facilities for the growing colony, and that these efforts were largely missionary. That these schools did not multiply more rapidly, as among the towns of New England, was because of the scattered agricultural population, and not from lack of appreciation of the largest and best culture. But the conditions making it impossible to have so many town schools, the want was largely supplied by the employment of private tutors.

Nor was the first of these schools planted in the East, as has been persistently claimed. The first free grammar-schools —that is, schools in which Latin was taught, and which were supported, in part, at least, by the proceeds of land, etc.

—were established in Charlestown, Va., in 1621; in Boston, 1636, in Salem, 1641; and in most towns of New England within a few years after their settlement.

RECITING LESSONS FOR THE SCHOOL MASTER

I wish, in this connection, to correct a false statement of history and deny the unfounded deduction from such misrepresentation. The reply of Sir William Berkeley, the governor, to a petition of the Virginia colonists has been quoted as the educational expression of the "lords of plantations" themselves, and made to type all the colonies of the South. They are represented as not only being indifferent, but hostile to general education, while the pioneers of New England were giving equal and careful attention to the school and the Church. Now, as a matter of fact, the colonists presented a petition to the governor, Sir William Berkeley, praying that liberal and general provision be made for the education of their children. That petition the upstart of a governor, recently arrived from England, resisted and denied in the following language:

WILLIAM BERKELEY

I thank God there are no schools nor printing, and I hope we shall not have them these one hundred years; for learning has brought disobedience and heresy and sects into the world, and printing has divulged them, and libels against the best government. God keep us from both!

Now, so far from this being the sentiment of the colonists, their "apathy or hostility in regard to popular schools," as one writer states it, was the formal denial of their earnest request. But the intelligent and far-seeing pioneers were not to be foiled in their educational demands, and steps were at once taken to establish William and Mary College.

Education in Maryland and The Carolinas

In Maryland and the Carolinas early legislative efforts were made "to establish schools for the convenient instruction of youth," and taxes were levied for their maintenance. The first constitution of Georgia provided that every county should "establish and keep a school at the public expense."

WILLIAM AND MARY COLLEGE

The preamble of the act establishing the first free school in Charleston, S. C., set forth "the necessity that a free school be erected for the instruction of youth in grammar and other arts and sciences, and also in the principles of the

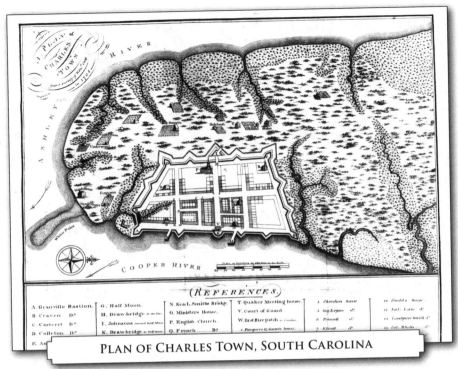

PLAN OF CHARLES TOWN, SOUTH CAROLINA

Christian religion; and that several well-disposed Christians, by their last will, had given several sums of money for the founding of a free school." It was provided, also, that the teacher "should be of the religion of the Church of England, and capable of teaching the Latin and Greek languages." Instructors were legally enjoined to see that the children "receive in their tender years that sense of religion which may render it the constant principle of their lives and actions."

Early Education in The Georgia Colony

The first school established in Georgia was by the Moravians, and was chiefly designed for the religious instruction of the Indians. The second was the famous Orphan House, built by the eloquent George Whitefield, intended to meet "the educational wants of the plantation." It was the great ambition of the wonderful preacher to make that estate "a seat and nursery of sound learning and religious education."

THE ORPHAN HOUSE

An interesting volume might be written on the "Famous Academies of America." Equally with the great colleges do they deserve historic recognition. But the story of every famous academy would be the life of its great teacher, who, in almost every instance, was a scholarly and self-denying minister of the gospel.

In referring to the fact that secondary instruction in America owes almost everything to religion, Dr. Baird shows also its special indebtedness to ministers of the gospel. Writing as late as 1843, the distinguished historian says:

> A large proportion of the grammar-schools and academies in the United States, whether incorporated or not, are under the direction and instruction of ministers of the gospel of different evangelical denominations. These ministers, in some cases, devote their whole time to the work of academical instruction. In other cases they also have the charge of a church or congregation, and as they perform the double duties of pastor and head of a grammar-school, they have usually an assistant teacher in the latter.

But, if possible, even more remarkable is the religious genesis of American colleges. For more than two hundred years almost every collegiate institution in the land owed its existence purely to religious motives, and was under the immediate control of some religious denomination. And the few established independently or by the state have relied upon Christian sympathy for support, and most of them have been presided over by devout ministers carrying the credentials of the Church of God.

Harvard College, the first institution for the promotion of higher education in the American colonies, was born of religious convictions. The colonists said: "It is an object near our hearts to have an able and learned ministry when those of the present age are laid in their graves." And the location of the institutions was determined by the same sacred consideration. Cambridge was selected, as the records show, because

JOHN HARVARD

"of the energy and searching character of Mr. Shepherd's preaching, and his skill in detecting errors." It's founder was a minister of the gospel—the Rev. John Harvard, whose name it bears—and to it he generously gave one-half of his estate, 800 pounds, and his library of three hundred and twenty volumes. The mottoes upon two of the ancient seals of the college are *In gloriam Christo* and

Christo et Ecclesiae. As indicating the jealous concern for the spiritual culture of the college, this was adopted among the early rules:

> Let every student be plainly instructed and earnestly pressed to consider well that the main end of his life and studies is to know God and Jesus Christ, which is eternal life, and, therefore, to lay Christ in the bottom as the only foundation of all sound knowledge and learning.

JOHN LEVERETT

It is a significant fact that during the first one hundred years of Harvard's history a little more than *three-sevenths* of its graduates were ministers of the gospel. And for the first one hundred and thirty-four years of its existence every President was a minister except one, the Hon. John Leverett, A.M., F.R.S., who served from 1707 to 1725, a period of eighteen years.

The second institution for advanced learning in the colonial period was William and Mary College, in Virginia, established in 1693. But that was not the first effort to plant such a school in that inviting section. Shortly after the Jamestown colonists landed and provided humble houses for their protection from the storms of winter and the heat of summer, a movement was inaugurated looking to the establishment of a college. It was to have an ambitious name—the "University of Henrico"—and ten thousand acres of land were laid off for an endowment. The Bishop of London heartily approved the worthy project, and

gave to it the munificent sum of 1,000
pounds. The Rev. Mr. Bargrave, the
clergyman at Henrico, donated his
library. And, as preparatory to this
larger enterprise, plans were devised
for building an academic school at
St. Charles City, to be known as the
East India School, in honor of the
officers and crew of an East India ship,
who made to it the first and largest
contribution. But these praiseworthy
enterprises, conceived of a true missionary spirit, came to
an untimely and tragic end by the terrible Indian massacre of
March, 1622. And so frequent were these savage wars, and so
many were the disasters to the struggling colony, that years
of disappointment had to pass before the ardent dream of the
early cavaliers was realized.

DR. JAMES BLAIR

In 1660 the Colonial Assembly passed an act "for the
establishment and endowment of a college," but not until the
coming of another minister, the Rev. Dr. James Blair, twenty-
eight years thereafter, did the movement find a successful
champion. The statement is that he "was deeply affected by
the low state of learning and piety in the colony, and, as the
most effective means of elevating both, resolved, if possible, to
secure the establishment of a college." Under his leadership
active measures were inaugurated, the religious purpose
of the movement being heartily seconded by the colonists,
who resolved "that for the advance of learning, education
of youth, supply of the ministry, and promotion of piety
there be land taken upon purchases for a college and free
school, and that there be, with as much speed as may be

convenient, housing erected thereon for entertainment of students and scholars." The governor and council headed a subscription which soon amounted to 2,500 pounds, and Dr. James Blair was commissioned to visit England in its behalf. The General Assembly, in making request for a royal endowment of the proposed college, stated that it was "to the end that the Church of Virginia may be furnished with a seminary for ministers of the gospel, and that the youth may be piously educated in good letters and manners, and that the Christian faith may be propagated amongst the Western Indians to the glory of Almighty God."

WILLIAM III

Their Majesties, William and Mary, received Dr. Blair most cordially, endorsed the enterprise most heartily, and the crown gave him 2,000 pounds and twenty thousand acres of land and a penny a pound on tobacco exported from Virginia and Maryland." The Colonial Assembly gave, as the statute read, "a duty on furs for its plentiful endowment," and Jefferson says that it also gave "a duty on liquors imported." So that "from these sources it received upward of 3,000 pounds *communibus annis*." The charter was granted February 14, 1692, the Bishop of London being appointed Chancellor; Dr. James Blair, President; and, in honor of

MARY II

their Majesties, was given the name of *William and Mary. The professors were to be members of the Church of England, and all students were to be taught the catechism.*

Yale College was founded by the Congregationalists, in response to a formal action by a synod of the churches held at New Haven in 1698, and was afterward given its name in honor of Elihu Yale, of London, governor of the East India Company, who made to the institution a generous donation. In the preamble of the charter granted by the Colonial Legislature, the high spiritual aims of the devout projectors is thus stated:

ELIHU YALE

> Several well disposed and Publick spirited Persons, of their sincere Regard to & zeal for upholding & Propagating of the Christian Protestant Religion by a succession of Learned & Orthodox men, have expressed by Petition their earnest desires that full Liberty and Privilege be granted unto certain Undertakers for the founding, suitably endowing, & ordering a Collegiate School within his Majties Colony of Connecticut, wherein Youth may be instructed in the Arts & Sciences, who through the blessing of Almighty God may be fitted for Public employment both in Church and Civil State.

And with exceeding jealous care did the ministers of Connecticut guard and guide the orthodox teachings of that college destined to such a magnificent history. Every President of the college for a hundred years was a minister of the gospel, and only a few times to the present has that apostolic succession been interrupted.

These were among the rules of Yale College in 1720:

> Seeing God is the giver of all wisdom, every scholar, besides private or secret prayer, wherein all we are bound to ask wisdom, shall be present morning and evening at public prayer in the hall at the accustomed hour, which is to be ordinarily at six of the clock in the morning, from the tenth of March to the tenth of September, and then again to the tenth of March at sunrising, at between four and five of the clock, all the year long.

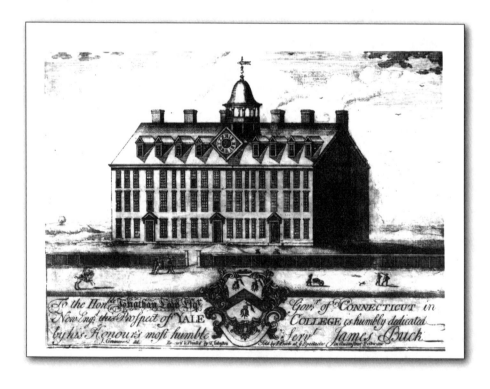

No scholar shall use the English tongue in the collegiate school with his fellow scholars unless he be called to public exercises proper to be attended in the tongue, but scholars in their chambers and when they are together shall talk Latin.

Columbia College, known until 1784 as King's College, was founded by the Episcopalians. The early Presidents were largely supported by Trinity Church, being made assistant rectors of the same. In 1735 Trinity Church granted to the college a valuable piece of ground, and among the conditions stipulated was "that the President should always be a member of the Episcopal Church, and that the college prayers should be drawn from the Prayer Book. The consideration was ten shillings and an annual rental of a peppercorn."

KING'S COLLEGE SHIELD

But into the detailed history of America's early colleges, the limits of this discussion will not allow me to enter. Each contains most valued facts in support of my earnest contention. These bare statements confined to the colonial period of America, and embracing all the early collegiate privileges provided for the people, indicate the measures and source of our indebtedness, and are eloquently suggestive of the educational policy that should be sacredly conserved:

College	When Founded	By Whom
Harvard	1638	Congregationalists
William and Mary	1693	Episcopalians
Yale	1700	Congregationalists
Princeton	1746	Presbyterians
University of Pennsylvania	1747	Individuals and State
Columbia	1759	Episcopalians
Brown University	1764	Baptists
Rutgers	1770	Dutch Reformed.
Dartmouth	1770	Congregationalists.
Hampden Sydney	1775	Presbyterians

The University of Pennsylvania, the first institution in the United States not established by a Christian denomination, was largely indebted to the Churches for moral and financial support, and has always been under Christian control. Prof. Thompson, an alumnus and a member of the Faculty of

BROWN UNIVERSITY CAMPUS

that historic institution, thus refers to its history, "Even my own university, the first in America without any definite denominational connection, owed to the Christian ministry both the ablest of its teachers and the bulk of its students, and it recognized its close relations to the Churches by giving the senior minister of each denomination a seat in its Board of Trustees, while the city churches took up a collection every year for its support;" and Dr. Dorchester, in his history of *Christianity in the United States*, says that the University of Pennsylvania, when first established, gathered its resources "by subscription in England, South Carolina, Jamaica, and Philadelphia. Thomas Penn, one of the proprietors, was the largest contributor."

And in the charter of your University of Georgia, granted in 1785, these words occur: "All officers appointed to the instruction and government of the university shall be of the Christian religion." Alas that in these latter days they should have been stricken from that time-honored instrument!

The curricula of these early colleges gave prominence to theology and the study of the Holy Scriptures in the original languages. "At Harvard, Hebrew, Chaldee, and Syriac, as well as New Testament Greek and catechetical theology, were taught.... In Yale, from the first, the Hebrew of the Old Testament was translated into Greek, and the Latin New Testament into Greek at the beginning of every recitation. The Assembly's Catechism in Latin was recited every Saturday evening; Ames's *Medulla Theologiae* Saturday mornings, and his *Cases of Conscience* Sunday mornings. There were also, from an early day, college lectures in ecclesiastical history, and a professorship in divinity. At Harvard one had to be able to render the originals of the Old and New Testaments and resolve them logically, withal being of godly life and conversation, in order to receive the first degree."

The standard of scholarship in those colonial colleges was, with the exception of mathematics, not low. Their founders and first promoters being graduates of Oxford and Cambridge, they sought to make scholars here equal to those in the old world. The following requirement for entrance into the first college class at Harvard would hardly be insisted upon by any university of today:

> When any scholar is able to understand Tully, or such like classical author, extempore and make and speak true Latin in verse and prose; . . . and decline perfectly the paradigms of nouns and verbs in the Greek tongue, let him then, and not before, be capable of admission into the college.

These facts are given to show that the only friends of higher education in the early days of America were Church people, and it was Church money that established and endowed those institutions. Not only so, but almost every professors' chair for many years was filled by a minister of the gospel. They were our national educators. The academies and "old field schools" were nearly all taught by clergymen.

But in these latter days we hear much of "liberal thought," and a growing demand of the people that their sons shall be educated in non-denominational institutions—colleges unfettered by "narrow orthodoxy" and uncontrolled by Christian Churches. Let us see if this is so. In the admirable and exhaustive report of the United States Commissioner of Education, in 1884, I find these figures:

Total number of colleges 370
Denominational colleges 309
Undenominational colleges. 61

Of the undenominational colleges, 23 are state institutions.

Denominational students. 25,948
Undenominational students 6,819
                                        ‾‾‾‾‾‾‾
Total. 32,767

In 1830 denominational colleges were 71 per cent of the whole; in 1884 they were 83 per cent. In 1830 the denominational students were 74 per cent of the whole; in 1884 they were 79 per cent.

So that according to these facts the demand seems rather for the increased care of the Churches—that the training of American youth shall be under the guidance of the Christian conscience, and under the immediate supervision of the Christian denominations. This accentuates the duty of the Church, and is an eloquent appeal for redoubled effort and increased vigilance and improved equipment.

The history of education in the American commonwealth abundantly sustains the statement of Dr. Candler that "from Harvard, the oldest, down to the latest established, there is hardly an institution of learning in the country that did not have its birth in and its growth from Christianity." Under the fostering care of the Church they were built—every stone "laid in denominational mortar." That man, therefore, is innocent of the elementary facts of history who declaims against or seeks to undervalue education by the Church; and that legislative assembly evidences a lamentable lack of acquaintance with the sacred spirit by which our early government was baptized which discriminates against

WARREN CANDLER

the educational institutions of the Church—the nurseries of our purest patriotism, the guardians of our dearest rights, the strongholds of our nation's destiny. Whatever may be one's opinion as to the sphere of public education, the State can not ignore or deny its educational indebtedness to the Church without peril and scandal. The more friendly the attitude of the State to the institutions of the Church and the more liberal her policy in fostering the same, the more perfectly will she safeguard the forces that insure her increasing prosperity. The State has no worse enemy than the small politician who, under the plea of guarding the institutions of the commonwealth, would embarrass, by hostile legislation, the schools of learning fostered by the Christian Church.

The cry of liberalism in education is really the first note of the Commune. It is the spirit which, if left to grow, will pull down the Vendome column and lay ruthless hands upon the ark of the Lord. Christian education is not narrow. It does not fetter thought, but emancipates mind. It does not impede investigation, but flings wide the doors of the largest mental hospitality, and gives the broadest commission to "intermeddle with all knowledge." For the small demagogue, whose cry is liberalism, and who has "no language but a cry," we ought to have the commiseration due to congenital innocence.

The maxim of the Puritans, "The proper nurse for Moses is Moses' mother," might be applied most aptly to the cause of education in the American commonwealth. Our school and college systems are the creations of Christianity. It was not until the Christian Church fought and won the battle for education that the world discovered its vast excellence and counted its institutions worthy of munificent endowment.

Victor Hugo has said that "he who opens the door of the schoolhouse closes the door of the jail." That depends on who keeps the school and what is taught there. The schoolhouse may become a place for polishing fiends and graduating outlaws. It is not the number but the character of our schools; not how many children attend, but who teaches them, and what they are taught, that type and measure their influence for good.

I do not think it extravagant to insist that the right education of American childhood is to determine the destiny of this great republic. There is profound philosophy and historic truth in that old proverb which says: "What you sow in the school you reap in the nation." Correct principles sown in the soil of the young mind, cultivated by wise, well-equipped teachers, and ripened by the sun of a gracious Providence, will produce a manhood and womanhood that will sacredly preserve the past and guarantee the glory of the future.

VICTOR HUGO

Charles B. Galloway
"Citizen, Patriot, Publicist"

From William Larkin Duren
Charles Betts Galloway: Orator, Preacher, and
"Prince of Christian Chivalry" (1932)

HAVING DISCUSSED BISHOP Galloway from the standpoint of his religious and ecclesiastical relations, it is now in order to give some attention to the more general interests and efforts of his life. His activities were not confined to what might be termed wholly ecclesiastical lines; but he gave much attention to social and philanthropic matters—broader interests which we classify as duties of citizenship. There was no interest of community building, no problem of social righteousness and no political movement to which he did not contribute either directly or indirectly. He did not accept the captious limitations so often insisted upon for ministers; for he believed that all legitimate civic obligations are entirely consistent with the divine calling of a minister; and he accepted it as his duty to do whatever he might to secure such adjustment of social conditions and political life as should best promote the happiness and the welfare of the people as a whole. To express it in his own thought: His first relation was that of a citizen, and he did not vacate that relation nor abrogate its responsibilities when he became a minister. It is true that he denied the right of any minister to become a political partisan, on the ground that his ministerial commission was to every individual; but he was equally positive that this political inhibition did not subtract from his obligation to promote righteousness, justice and truth as constructive factors of civilization and progress. Holding such opinion, therefore, he gave himself freely and conscientiously to many matters of public interest and importance; and by his leadership in various moral reforms he added to the luster of the fame which he achieved as a minister.

It would be impossible to crowd the discussion of his activities as a citizen into the limits of a single chapter, and we reserve certain important and allied subjects for separate treatment. Among such questions, are: his advocacy of temperance, interest in race relations, and work for the promotion of education. In the present chapter, we propose to discuss the fundamental principles and attitudes which entered into the making of his character as a citizen—the ideas which gave direction to his work for civic righteousness, and inspired the political aspects of his life and labors. In these principles we shall find the connecting link between his spiritual vocation and his more secular activities; and we shall discover the motives which secured a sequence in all that he did—that made him a Christian craftsman in every interest of his life.

The critics of Bishop Galloway were not more generous in their attitude toward his social ideals and his stand for public righteousness than are their successors whom we know today. They sought to discredit his efforts by attributing to him secret ambitions and conceits. But the complete answer to such ungenerous disparagement of his motive and conduct is the prayer which he offered at the opening of the Mississippi Constitutional Convention in 1890. The greatness of the occasion would have tempted an ambitious man to indicate his desires, and a conceited man to exploit his gifts; but such indications are entirely absent from that invocation. It is a model of devoutness, directness and good taste. It contains no ornate sentence fashioned for the ear of the vain man, and it does not refer specifically to any major issue with which the Convention was faced. It was an earnest plea for Divine wisdom, guidance and support on behalf of the Convention which held in its power the political fortunes of a great State, and the social destiny of more than a million souls. His plea for grace, through which the members might be able to recognize this great responsibility, was eloquent in its simplicity and apostolic in its sincerity and fervor. It is a faithful portrayal of the heart of the man who uttered it, and a key to his effectiveness and popularity as a leader in the life of that commonwealth.

Bishop Galloway believed that citizenship is the practical every-day application of Christianity; and that one's interest in public affairs should be deepened and intensified by his faith and Christian experience. This is not an idea concerning which we need to offer conjecture, for his public utterances abound in sentiments which leave no doubt as to his thought on the subject. For example, he said: "That is a cheap conception of the Christian religion which limits the sphere of its operation to what has been called 'other worldliness'—to a ceaseless contemplation of and concern for the things that are heavenly. It takes in the whole man—the entire sweep of his being—and is concerned for everything that affects his character and destiny from daily bread to eternal life."[1] In this statement, he asserts that Christian responsibility includes everything from the needs of the present moment to the fulfillment of man's immortal hope. And it is certain that he did not accept any interpretation of Christianity that might place a barrier, political or social, in the way of the complete fulfillment of his spiritual task.

In another connection, he made more specific statement emphasizing his belief in an unrestricted ethical responsibility and liberty for the Christian. "We should abolish, and forever banish," he says, "the false distinction between the sacred and the secular. The functions of citizenship are as sacred as the songs of Zion. The ballot is as holy as the Book of Common Prayer. The same law of duty controls in the service of country and in the conventicles of the sanctuary; in the balls of state and at the chancel of the house of God."[2] In this address, he was not speaking to a group of Christian men, as such; he was telling the Press Association of Mississippi that he did not submit to a limitation of his activity that might help to defeat the gospel that he was commissioned to preach. He frequently said that he did not believe in two consciences, one for politics and one for prayer-meeting; one for the ballot box and one for the church pew. In other words, he did not think that a man's ethical and moral obligations were changed by the company he happened to be in. He said: "The duties of citizenship and Christianity are not in conflict. No fealty to God can be disloyalty to country. Nor can patriotic service to country be infidelity to God."[3] He believed that the duties of citizenship rest upon the same moral and spiritual foundation as do the claims of the church, and that there can be no reduction of the   privileges and obligations of the citizen without doing violence to every public interest and to the kingdom of God as well.

The Nashville *Tennesseean* summed up his political position thus, "He knew that the kingdom of God, while not of this world, is nevertheless, in this world and must find here the sphere of its development and the field of its achievement."

But, however insistent upon his freedom in all the legitimate activities of political life, there were certain alignments which he held to be inconsistent with the ministerial vocation. He said: "Every minister of Christ should be a patriot, but never a partisan politician. The miter and the crown should never encircle the same brow. The crozier and the scepter should never be wielded by the same hand."[4] On another occasion, he said: "I give it as my matured opinion that the church, as such, can not ally herself to any political party, though every plank in its platform be in accord with the sermon on the Mount." Many times and for many reasons efforts were made to dissuade him from a rigid adherence to this position, but only to evoke a new declaration of his conviction on that subject. His stand was not a concession, a matter of expediency, but was loyalty to principle and, therefore, not something to be modified or abandoned at will.

There are those who will be disposed to applaud the counsel of Bishop Galloway respecting ministerial participation in partisan politics; but such should not overlook the fact that his counsel was in no case the denial of the minister's duty as a citizen, but it was in reality a declaration of political independence. He said, "No flat of caucus or convention can bind or unbind a Christian's conscience."[5] The farthest thing from his thought was to counsel neutrality on any moral issue. So he said: "Sectarianism should never enter politics, but religion everywhere and always. The churches should have no political creed, but individual Christians should not be without one, clearly defined and conscientiously embraced. Every citizen a politician, and every politician a religious, God-fearing man, would make this an ideal republic of supernal strength and beauty. To approximate it should be our prayer and effort."[6] He did not believe that the ministry of the church could fulfill its true mission, keep itself unspotted from the world, and, at the same time, serve the partisan aims of a political party. But he was certainly not meaning to give comfort to those who would thrust the Christian Church and its ministry out of the way, in order to achieve their selfish and corrupt ambitions. In an article written from Vicksburg, Mississippi, about 1880, he made reply to the warnings of politicians against mixing politics and religion, saying: "If acted upon to its fullest logical conclusion, it would bankrupt the morals of society and prostrate our grand republic in the dust." He declared that the doctrine which says: "A man must have two consciences and two sets of principles, the one to obey his God and the other to serve his country . . . slanders God and degrades manhood."[7]

So far from being willing to abandon politics to men of the world, he said: "There is an ethical *obligation upon every citizen to take an active part in public affairs.*"[8] He held the franchise to be one of the most sacred privileges and responsibilities of citizenship, saying: "In republican governments, founded upon and sustained by popular will, it is a Christian citizen's highest duty to use the power of the ballot in the interest of good government."[9] But, much as he favored the use of the ballot, he had no use for "agrarianism," and he lamented such a spirit either in politics or religion. He planted himself upon a Christian interpretation of citizenship and the use of its privileges to secure and maintain good government.

It must not be supposed, however, that Bishop Galloway's convictions on this subject were exhausted in theories, or that they ended in a formal expression of his choices on election day. He was outspoken in his demand for a citizenship that should itself be a keeper of the laws of the land. In a day when summary justice was meted out at the hands of irresponsible mobs, he said:

"To correct this evil, enthrone the sanctity of law, and respect for constituted authority and human life, we need a social, moral revolution. . . . The spirit of killing must be stamped out.

"Every act of unauthorized justice makes each participant ever after reckless of human life. His one desperate deed, however dastardly the crime he would avenge, gives him a contempt for all law and its proper administration. He sneers at its tedious processes and thirsts for a summary enforcement. And for fear that some violent hand, with a ready trigger, will avenge his own bloody work, he becomes himself a walking arsenal, with an acute car and eye for every sound and motion. The homicides of our section are traceable to the lynching spirit of a few years ago, too often condoned, if not applauded.

"There are no circumstances when lynch law is allowable. Its effect in deterring criminal classes from like deeds is lost in its ruinous, deadly influence upon the participants themselves. The forms of law should be preserved inviolate, and its administrators held to a strict account. The argument in favor of summary punishment—that law, in its ordinary processes, is too tedious and uncertain-is mischievous and misleading. We can not secure better administration by becoming outlaws ourselves. We defeat the ends of justice by taking its cause in private, ruthless, unauthorized hands. The greatest enemies of the peace and security of a community are those who constitute themselves its guardians and champions."[10]

This demand for law observance included not only those who went to the extent of committing crimes, but those, also, who sought, for whatever reason, to evade the unpleasant duty of making law enforcement effective through service on grand juries and trial juries. On this point he uttered no uncertain sound: "Men of character and active business have betrayed the dearest interests of the commonwealth by pleading frivolous excuses to escape the most responsible duty of an American citizen."[11] He added to this charge the further statement that, "The most contemptible and vicious man in society is the professional juror—unless it is the jury fixer." These quotations show that he felt that the hope of securing a righteous administration of laws lies in the repressive influence of men of character and public prestige measuring up to their civic obligations as jurors.

Bishop Galloway was not more a believer in the repressive influence of good citizenship than he was emphatic in his demand for "constructive statesmanship." In one of his greatest addresses on public matters, he said: "We want builders rather than destroyers—leaders not objectors—the hammer stroke instead of the bugle note. We want commanders who will not only give warning of the dangerous course to be shunned, but will point out the way of progress to be pursued. The destructive critic has his place, and is not without definite value, but he leaves no monuments—only ruins. Criticism, when discriminating and sincere, is wholesome and necessary, but becomes pernicious when it hardens into a habit. My ardent ambition for the South is, that she will not sit forever on the Opposition benches, but develop a generation of mighty leaders of creative and constructive genius, each with all the seven lamps of architecture in his strong brave hand, building and painting for the eternities."[12] With all the prescience of true political philosophy, he was pointing the way of progress and stability in governmental affairs.

He scorned the spirit and method of the demagogue as being subversive of political prosperity and public morals. "The duty," he said, "of one aspiring to political leadership is to *think* for his people and courageously point out the path of national honor and prosperity. His high aim should be not to cunningly watch for favoring breezes of popular passion, but heroically and sincerely give direction to public opinion. That which differentiates the demagogue from the patriot-statesman, is the measure and flippancy of his fair promises, with never a scruple as to the infamy of his deception or the tragedy of his country's humiliation. Any man is essentially dishonest who will advocate measures of dangerous, or even doubtful utility, in order to win votes and ride into power."[13] He knew that the policy of the demagogue would mean a continuous change of administration, solve no problem of state and meet none of the changing conditions of life, and only serve to fill the measure of unworthy ambitions at the expense of the economic and moral life of the people.

He anticipated a peril to American institutions which the public at large has been slow to comprehend—that is, the cheapening of American citizenship by the introduction of elements which are constitutionally at variance with our thinking, and lack sympathy with our institutions—who do not even speak the English language. He said: "I am in most perfect accord with the sentiment that *every man who lives in America should be an American citizen and speak the English language.* There should be no aliens on our shores and no foreign tongue in our national speech."[14] These words do not mean that he was illiberal toward the thousands of foreign peoples who are attracted to our shores by the wonderful opportunities offered, but that he wanted to keep inviolate the privilege and opportunity of American citizenship for other millions who would continue to seek our much favored land. He was ambitious that we should always have something of inestimable value to offer to aspiring people beyond the seas.

His idea of immigration regulation was no projection of maudlin sentiment, and his position was in sharp and striking contrast with the visionary benevolence of some social leaders in that particular. He gave expression to a very sane view when he said: "I verily believe that we have worked that old idea of the 'asylum for the oppressed' too far. Nine hundred and twenty-one thousand persons coming from Europe in one year—from Austria-Hungary, from Italy, from Russia, and other countries, strain to the very utmost the assimilating power of our social and national institutions, and the energies of the Church of God."[15] After twenty-five years of grappling with this question and the issues which have arisen out of it, the wisdom of that pronouncement can hardly be questioned.

Although he took no part in practical politics, as such, it is probably true that his political influence was as great as that of any other man in Mississippi. Judge Edward Mayes said of him: "He had in politics a certain good influence, which he freely used, and which was potent for the right."[16] Chancellor Kirkland, of Vanderbilt University, said: "His influence as a citizen was conspicuous in his own State, where he was accorded the distinctive title of 'The First Citizen of Mississippi.'"[17] His authority as a civic leader did not originate in his ecclesiastical credentials, neither was it brought about by his refraining from participation in partisan politics, but it was due to his own Christian character and convictions. He never took counsel of his audience as to what he should say, not that he ignored their feelings or the proprieties of an occasion, but rather that he was supremely interested in truth and righteousness. In the South, he spoke fearlessly and directly on the subject of social injustice, race crimes and political corruption. In Michigan, he delivered his address on Jefferson Davis, "without modifying any judgment or shading down any expression."[18] He defended the character of Mr. Davis and maintained the Constitutional position of his own people.

Bishop Galloway took high ground on the subject of political and party morality. During the early years of his ministry, he wrote: "Platforms are but as dust under our feet, if their advocates are wanting in manly honor and scrupulous fidelity."[19] More than a quarter of a century later he says: "In political, as in personal conduct, there is a right and wrong, and by that divine and universal standard men and measures must stand or fall. It is an eternal decree from which there is neither exemption nor exception. And no brilliancy of genius or splendor of achievement or conspicuousness of position can save a man, lacking in moral integrity, from the merited and irreparable condemnation of history." In the same address, he places party morality above theories of government which inspire platform pronouncements: "Far more important than governmental theories or party policies or campaign issues is the moral quality of the measures we advocate and the moral character of the men we elevate." Also: "In the drafting of platforms we need *honest* rather than *skillful* hands, and the declaration of fundamental principles rather than the enunciation of paramount issues. A platform is to stand on and not to get in on. It should not be a snare for votes, but a creed of faith—not a bag for game, but a code of conduct. The question should be, not will an issue be popular, but is it right. The strength of party platforms and political programs is not in their appeal to the people's discontent, but in the encouragement of their larger hopes."[20]

Another question of governmental honesty with which he stirred the State of Mississippi, was his attack upon the repudiation of the Planters' Bank bonds of 1830–1803 and the Mississippi Union Bank bonds of 1838. The validity of these bonds had been affirmed by a decision of the Supreme Court of Mississippi, and nearly a hundred years had passed since the act of repudiation, but the outlawing of $8,500,000 of the State's obligations was so utterly at variance with the instincts of his soul that he could not rest under the odium of such a transaction without making a protest. He said: "The perpetual humiliation of Mississippi is the fact that the word REPUDIATION was ever attached to her great name. And through all the years to come, whatever the apology or explanation of that ever-to-be-lamented act, the State can not escape a measure of disgrace. The statute of limitations can never run against genuine honesty."[21] He drew the fire of every politician and taxeconomizing citizen of the State, but none of them dared to defend the act of repudiation. They insisted that restitution at that day would pile tax burdens on innocent shoulders, and they were willing to forget the indictment: "Repudiation—a word that contains the very exhaustion of disgrace and disgust."

In 1876, Bishop Galloway visited Washington City and was in the House of Representatives at the hour of prayer. His note on that occasion may help to cure the pessimism of some and curb the optimism of others of our times. He wrote: "The House was opened with prayer by the chaplain—an Episcopal clergyman in full canonicals. Such shameless neglect of divine worship I never witnessed before—a few stood up, a few bowed their heads, while the great mass looked on in not very quiet indifference. Prayer on such occasions is mere form, without heart or solemnity."[22] He was not deceived by the forms of religious devotion, for it was all too manifest that their hearts were not in the thing that was being done. He was not discouraged, however, by such a show of indifference and irreverence; for he knew that back of even the formal acknowledgment which they were making was a latent spiritual energy to which appeal could always be made. He was not cast down by slow progress or even temporary defeats in the moral crusades in which he engaged; for his doctrine was that moral reforms may be checked and retarded, but they never turn backward.

Bishop Galloway was a loyal Southerner—devoted to Southern ideals and a defender of Southern traditions and Southern character. He was the embodiment of the chivalry of the Old South and the enthusiastic herald of the New South. He was an unusual blending of the traditional and the progressive spirit, and more unusual in that he never allowed either tendency to dominate his thought and conduct. He was claimed by all parties and trusted by all factions, not because he was guilty of any effort to deceive or mislead; but because he convinced all of his integrity and his purpose to act upon the highest plane of right and honor. An example of his quick and able defense of Southern character is a reply which he made to an attack upon Southern womanhood by Dr. C. H. Fowler in the New York *Christian Advocate*, in March, 1880. After reviewing misstatements of fact and paying his respects to the malignant spirit of the editorial, he concludes: "No doubt away down in his heart of hearts, the suggestion will come up, 'I was thinking of Cincinnati next May, the General Conference in session there, and the possibility of my winning the mantle of Bishop Haven.'"[23] The reference was to the fact that Bishop Gilbert Haven had died and there would probably be additions to the Episcopacy, which may have been responsible for the injudicious outburst and the sectional bitterness of Dr. Fowler's utterance.

As the years passed, Bishop Galloway probably became very much less sectional in his own feelings, but not less Southern in his sympathies. Evidence of such sympathy appears in the deliverance:

"The nation has had enough of geographical politics. . . We have a right, therefore, to protest against being kept on perpetual probation. If the South contains a statesman with eminent qualifications for the Presidency of this great nation, there should be no hesitancy in urging his nomination and election."[24]

We are persuaded that this is a word of counsel which the Democratic Party might have heeded to its profit and which might have added greatly to its prestige in the nation.

After all, Southern as he was, the emphasis of his soul was upon the integrity and worth of the man who might be considered for place or power. He said: "But above all else let us put the emphasis upon *manhood*. The strength of every nation is measured by the quality of its citizenship. To no purpose is the country great if the men are small. On the other hand, great men are the incarnation of great principles, and they alone type and determine the destiny of nations and civilizations."[25] He desired no recognition for the South, except that to which it was justly entitled by reason of character and qualification for national leadership. He asked no political dole as a means of relieving Southern humiliation—rather that the South should clutch the prize to which it had title by virtue of its citizenship.

The greatness of Bishop Galloway, as a citizen, can not be discovered through either his phrases or his political philosophy. He had marvelous felicity of speech, and unusual discrimination in the use of figures for expressing his thought; but back of all that he said was an upstanding man whose veins were filled with red blood. In his public advocacy of moral and social issues, the chivalry of his soul lighted his face with the gleam of a patriot's devotion. It is easy to argue with one's self that the ideals of religion are moral preachments rather than expressions of reality and life; but to come face to face with a great soul changes such thoughts into accusers of one's own heart. Bishop Galloway was never greater than in the simple and unostentatious exhibition of political integrity and personal manhood.

His intellectual detachment was not revealed in a prolific evolving of new schemes and ideas—his mind was not of the jazz type. He took the world as he found it, and under his interpretations the drab relations of citizenship were charged into spiritual imperatives. He was too clear in his convictions and too acute in his judgment to be duped by the soft counsels of those who feigned an interest in his personal popularity. And he understood full well the wily schemes of those who would exempt political and social matters from all ecclesiastical interference or interpretation by the spirit and teaching of Jesus. He kept his heart and mind fixed upon "the kingdom of God and his righteousness," and to other things he was indifferent.

He understood the strain upon a man who would meet squarely the issues of citizenship—the responsibility for good government. He said that the strain on a man's courage to become a Christian in a land where it means social and political ostracism is one of the chief difficulties encountered in foreign missions. And, by plain implication, the home phase of that same problem is to continue to be Christian in the face of the opposition offered by every selfish and even sensuous interest that seeks to lay its corrupting hand upon the political life of the world. Bishop Galloway proved himself to be equal to every test. He was a great ecclesiastic, but a great citizen as well—Christ's man in the fullest sense.

Notes

1. Sermon, *Duties of Christian Citizenship.*
2. Address, *The Ethics of Politics*, 1907.
3. Sermon, *The Duties of Citizenship.*
4. Sermon, *The Duties of Citizenship.*
5. Article, *The Clarion.* 1879.
6. Address, *The Ethics of Politics*, 1907.
7. Article, *The Clarion.*
8. Address, *The Ethics of Politics.*
9. Sermon, *Duties of Christian Citizenship.*
10. Editorial, *Unbalanced Justice* (July 12, 1883).
11. Sermon, *Duties of Christian Citizenship.*
12. Address, *Dedication Mississippi State Capitol June 3, 1903).*
13. Address, *The Ethics of Politics*, 1907.
14. Manuscript Note.
15. Address, *Inter-Church Conference on Federation*, New York, 1906.
16. Mayes, *Mississippi Historical Society Papers*, 11:27.
17. Kirkland, *Memorial Address* (May 13, 1909).
18. Letter to J. R. Bingham (August 8, 1908).
19. Article in *The Clarion*, 1879.
20. Address, *The Ethics of Politics*, 1907.
21. Address, *The Ethics of Politics*, 1907.
22. Manuscript Notebook, 1876
23. Newspaper Article, 1880.
24. Address, *Dedication Mississippi State Capitol* (June 3, 1903).
25. Address, *Dedication Mississippi State Capitol* (June 3, 1903).